MAMMA TRAUMA

If It's Not One Thing,

It's Your Mother!

A Healing Guide

DALE BACH

Published by Awakening Joy Publishers

Cover design by Lan Gao.
Printed in the United States of America

MAMMA TRAUMA: If It's Not One Thing, It's Your Mother! A Healing Guide does not constitute medical or therapeutic advice for any medical or psychological condition. In the presence of any medical or psychological history, or symptoms of any type, please seek the care of a physician. The author and publisher do not assume any liability for damages of any kind resulting directly or indirectly from the implementation of information given in this book. Any application of the material in the following pages is at the reader's discretion and is the reader's sole responsibility.

For further information, visit my website at www.dalebach.com.

ISBN #978-0-9884754-0-3

With deep love I dedicate this book:

To all mothers and daughters who are on their journey of connecting to the Divine Mother within, and to every woman who is willing and ready to grow and step into their wholeness and remember their essence, which is love.

To my mother, Kitty, for giving me life and all the major opportunities to grow and get strong, for loving me the best she could, and for her fiery and spunky spirit.

To my sister V., for her love, support, and humor and for her amazing courage in her colorful individualization process.

To my beloved, beautiful daughters, Ingrid and Gretchen, for being the brave souls that they are and gracing me with their divine presence, innocence, and beauty, which allowed me to open my heart and transform the patterns of abuse; for inviting me into their adult lives with celebration, love, and gratitude; and for gifting and blessing me with the highest privilege of experiencing the miracle of unconditional love and the tremendous joy that is eternally activated in my life.

To Ingrid: The world should know what an incredible woman you are and the children you love and teach in your Kindergarten class are blessed beyond description to have you as their teacher. You are changing this world one child at a time. I am so proud that you are my daughter.

To Gretchen: My first supporter and cheerleader who encouraged me to tell my story to the world. You gave me confidence in the power of my story. You have such a beautiful sweetness about you. Who you are is a magnificent being of light and love. You, too, have made me so very proud to be your mother.

With deep love I dedicate this book:

To all mothers and daughters who are on their journey of connecting to the Divine Mother within, and to every woman who is willing and ready to grow and step into their wholeness and remember their essence, which is love.

To my mother, Kitty, for giving me life and all the major opportunities to grow and get strong, for loving me the best she could, and for her fiery and spunky spirit.

To my sister V., for her love, support, and humor and for her amazing courage in her colorful individualization process.

To my beloved, beautiful daughters, Ingrid and Gretchen, for being the brave souls that they are and gracing me with their divine presence, innocence, and beauty, which allowed me to open my heart and transform the patterns of abuse; for inviting me into their adult lives with celebration, love, and gratitude; and for gifting and blessing me with the highest privilege of experiencing the miracle of unconditional love and the tremendous joy that is eternally activated in my life.

To Ingrid: The world should know what an incredible woman you are and the children you love and teach in your Kindergarten class are blessed beyond description to have you as their teacher. You are changing this world one child at a time. I am so proud that you are my daughter.

To Gretchen: My first supporter and cheerleader who encouraged me to tell my story to the world. You gave me confidence in the power of my story. You have such a beautiful sweetness about you. Who you are is a magnificent being of light and love. You, too, have made me so very proud to be your mother.

Gratitude from the deepest part of my heart and soul:

A huge thank you and sincere appreciation to Tony Parinello for gently pushing me to pull the manuscript out of my garage and get it edited and published, for being my biggest fan, support, coach, friend, and mentor; and for believing in me and the importance of this work when I didn't.

I want to thank all my extraordinary editors for the parts they played in preparing this book.

Brandon Yusuf Toropov, thank you for your expertise, rigorous honesty and patience for helping me get to the other side of my darkest moments and coming out of it with humor and wit. For taking my stream of consciousness writing and making my stories readable and for making me look like a good writer.

Kaine Thompson, thank you for your remarkable editorial coaching which took my book to the next level, making sure my authentic voice was heard. You helped me put back what I thought I needed to take out and gave me the courage to own my voice and my story.

Ingrid Siss, a very heartfelt thank you for your loving support and wonderful encouragement while going through all of this to make sure it made sense and helping me "cross the t's and dot the i's".

Mo Rafael, thank you for taking an extremely rough first draft and making it look like a readable draft.

Elizabeth Powers, a big thank you for convincing me that my story could help others.

Ann Haug, thank you for your high standards of excellence and your ability to find and highlight the treasures of this book in the final editing stages. You're like an angelic God sent mid-wife who helped me birth this book.

Thank you, Vanessa Lua, my loyal and cheerful assistant, for keeping my office and affairs in order while I went through this process and for all you continue to do!

I also want to express my deepest gratitude to all of my beloved teachers and mentors who gave me the tools to heal and remember who I really am: Dr. Michael Bernard Beckwith, Neale Donald Walsch, Dr. Ron and Mary Hulnick, Dr. Leonard Laskow, Thich Nhat Hanh, Dr. Valerie Gersch, Dr. Jean Houston, Dr. Aline La Pierre, Abraham Esther and Jerry Hicks, Dr. Bob Gibson, Louise Hay, Colin Tipping and Tom Stone. For your music – Rickie Byars Beckwith and Karen Drucker.

Special acknowledgement to those who are listed below (in no particular order) for encouraging me, inspiring me, and believing in me: Gretchen Siss, Gloria Taylor Brown, Cher Slater Barlevi, Janet Robertson, Dr. Christine Horner, Patsy Wright-Maddock, Brent Maddock, Jim Farren, Cynthia Kersey, Libbe HaLevy, Lia Andrews, Judith Andrews, Rae A. Majors-Wildman, Richard McConnell, Debbie Hardesty, Laura Johnson, Judi Bryan, Tammi Sirotenko, Beth Banning, Neil Gibson, Roger Wetzel, Suzanne Finder, Judy and Ken Foster, Dale Ann Springer, Michele Burke, Dr. Benjo Masilungan, Eric Siss, Gene Borkan and Les Bach .

And to all of you who I may have forgotten to mention, I ask your forgiveness in advance because I could write a book just listing all those who have played a role in my life.

Praise for *MAMMA TRAUMA:*
If It's Not One Thing, It's Your Mother!

"Dale's training as an Agape Practitioner and wealth of knowledge on accelerated healing modalities make her an excellent resource for healing past hurts and breaking the chains that have been holding you back. The work she guides you through will be worth years of traditional therapy with results you can see and feel!"

Neale Donald Walsch
New York Times bestselling Author of *When Everything Changes, Change Everything: In a Time of Turmoil A Pathway to Peace*, best-selling author of *Conversations with God*. Also a Teacher on the movie <u>The Secret</u>.

~~~

"Through her profound inner practices as a spiritual practitioner, Dale Bach leads us from shame and dysfunction into a revolution in consciousness: reclaiming our self-empowerment, realizing our inner wholeness, and accepting ourselves into our own heart. Breathe, soften, and enjoy this tender and healing book."

Michael Bernard Beckwith
Author of Life Visioning
Founder, Agape International Spiritual Center

~~~

"An unforgettable personal journey offering important recovery lessons for all survivors of abuse of any kind."

Brandon Yusuf Toropov
Editor, owner of iWordSmith.com and author of several books including the *Complete Idiot's Guide* series

"MAMMA TRAUMA has compelling stories of the challenges of Dale Bach's life which opens your heart with deeper compassion invoking the Spirit within and inspiring you with hope and the healing tools to find freedom, forgiveness, and peace. I wholeheartedly endorse this book!"

Dr. Janette Marie Freeman
Author of *Why Did This Happen to Me Again?*

~~~

"Though horrifying at times, this book is bold and honest, a truly brave and inspiring, tender, loving, work of art. Dale Bach has written an indispensable book for those with "Mamma Trauma" - part memoir, part guidebook, to look deep inside ourselves and heal that innermost part of our soul. *MAMMA TRAUMA* has a message for all. I highly recommend it!"

Dr. Valerie Gersch, ND
Founder of Kalos Seminars International
Author of *Heal The Cause* and *A New Day In Healing*

~~~

"Dale's personal story of recovery from trauma will inspire you to take action towards the realization of your own vision for healthy, loving relationships. Allow her accelerated healing techniques to work for you to enrich your life in every way."

Mari Smith
Social Media Thought Leader, Speaker and Visionary
Author of *The New Relationship Marketing* and
Facebook Marketing: An Hour A Day

"Mother-daughter relationships can be complicated at times, and will influence the lives of both women forever. Dale takes the subject to a new level. Her book is written in a very candid way that grabs you and makes it hard to put down. It helps heal not only "Mamma Trauma", but all the little and big traumas we accumulate throughout our lives. The meditations and exercises are amazing, easy to follow and very effective."

Dr. Judith Andrews, DAOM, L.Ac.
Co-owner of Cinnabar Acupuncture Clinic and Spa

~~~

"I've known Dale as a powerful healer and teacher. I was moved by her experiences as a brave little girl, and the grace with which she transformed her story into a tool to help others in their healing. I recommend this book to anyone looking to heal their relationships and themselves. Beautiful and inspirational!"

Dr. Lia Andrews, DAOM, L.Ac.
Co-owner of Cinnabar Acupuncture Clinic and Spa,
author of *7 Times a Woman*

~~~

"The impact of mothering can last a lifetime. My Agape practitioner sister, Dale Bach, has written a beautiful and heart opening book that allows us to glimpse what she experienced in her childhood, how she transcended her trauma and simultaneously offers practices that will allow anyone to heal from any Mamma Trauma."

Wendy Silvers
Founder, Million Mamas Movement

"This is a gem of a book that doesn't leave anything on the table. It is one of the most revealing, emotionally raw and honest books I've read about a mother daughter relationship seeded in violence. The author's true story is compelling and she enlightens us to the life-long limiting beliefs and patterns that inevitably develop through trauma with one's mother. The author unabashedly invites you to see her shadow side that stemmed from violence and her struggle to be loved. The gift is that her naked honesty makes it easier for the reader to see their own shadow and this is an essential step in healing. Ultimately this book is about the healing process and the struggle to emerge whole. She gently guides us along the way with a menu of helpful processes. The reader is finally left with the insight that in order for us to heal ourselves, it is essential we heal the most primary relationship of our life. Thank God she has paved the way for us."

Elizabeth Powers

MSW, PSYCH-K Facilitator and Instructor

~ ~ ~

"There is an immediate, connected quality to working with Dale that feels almost bottomless. Now, after reading her new book, *MAMMA TRAUMA*, I know why: she has been on a rigorous journey of the soul, and, in reaching out for her own healing, has been the recipient of the teaching of many masters. Dale does not hold anything back. She gently, firmly and joyously meets you wherever you may be on your own path. She most generously gives her knowledge and spiritual gifts to enable you to make the paradigm shift that helps you let go of the darkness of trauma, restore your balance, reclaim a sense of wonder, and once again engage passionately with the world. Hers is a true gift of soul."

Janet Robertson

Foreword

As human beings on planet Earth, we all suffer traumas that need healing. Left unhealed, these emotional wounds can wreak havoc on our lives, causing emotional instability and torment that can sabotage and destroy our most important relationships, and our health. No one knows this better than Dale Bach. In this extraordinary guide to healing, *Mamma Trauma*, Dale shares her journey of overcoming her "traumatic" past.

Although her journey has been incredibly difficult, it transformed her into a gifted healer and skilled expert in an abundance of quick, effective healing techniques.

Dale's greatest desire is to help others. It is her deep love of humanity that inspired the courage it took to vulnerably share her story. Through telling her story, she knew she would be able to help others with significant traumas to heal too. This book is not about trauma, but rather an inspirational guide to healing.

As a board certified surgeon, I was taught a paradigm of healing that focused exclusively on the body as if it were a car going in for repairs. It didn't take very long to realize that this mechanically limited view of the human body doesn't associate much with health and healing.

In the past two decades we have been blessed with many ground breaking books about the science of emotional and mental influence on our health. Louise Hay, author of numerous books, including *You Can Heal Your Life*, was one of the first to describe the emotional issues underlying physical symptoms and illnesses. Carolyn Myss, medical intuitive and author of *Anatomy of the Spirit* expanded on the topic by describing disturbances in our energy systems known as chakras, caused by emotional issues which then lead to symptoms and disease in that area of the body. In order for one to heal physical symptoms and disease, the emotional issues must be addressed and healed.

Candace Pert, Ph.D., in her book *Molecules of Emotions*, was the first to document that every emotion we feel is associated with a release of chemical molecules into our body — providing scientific evidence that emotions have a direct effect on our physical bodies.

Emotional work is crucially important for our health. But, it can be very uncomfortable and tough—and therefore, many of us avoid it. It is easy, for instance, to take out a gallbladder—but much harder to dig deep into the issues of suppressed anger and resentment that congealed the gallstones. Take out the gallbladder and you may feel better initially, but eventually the unresolved anger and resentment will show itself again as another physical symptom, such as chronic pain or even cancer. Talk therapy made famous by Freud has benefits, but its success very much depends upon the skills of the therapist. It is generally slow, and may or may not lead to insights that result in healing.

Fortunately, in the past several decades numerous simple and effective techniques have been developed that can get to the root of emotional issues quickly, and help release and rewire the brain sometimes in just one session. For example, Eye Movement Desensitization and Reprocessing (EMDR) for post traumatic stress disorder and Psych-K, of which Dr. Bruce Lipton (Cellular Biologist and author of Biology of Belief) says, "The 'secret of life' is BELIEF. Rather than genes, it is our beliefs that control our lives. PSYCH-K is a set of simple, self-empowering processes to change your beliefs and perceptions that impact your life at a cellular level." These are two highly effective and rapid techniques.

From the outside looking in, no one would ever suspect that Dale Bach — a gregarious, energetic, and stunningly gorgeous woman — has healed from so many traumas. When you read this book, no doubt you will be left with the inspired feeling that I had. If this woman has been able to heal from all of her challenges, and now lives in grace, with a profound unshakable connection to the Divine, and a spirit so bright it lights up a room, then so can you.

Christine Horner, MD FACS
Nationally recognized surgeon, natural health expert, and author of *Waking The Warrior Goddess: Dr. Christine Horner's Program to Protect Against and Fight Breast Cancer*, winner of the IPPY award for Best Book in Health, Medicine and Nutrition 2006

My sister and I at ballet

Preface One: From my sister

Trauma is just another taboo; one that is never discussed openly by those that are subjected to it. We all have some trauma in our lives, whether from our early childhood, adolescence or adulthood.

When we are faced with trauma, family is supposed to be a place where we find love, comfort and support. However, when family is the source of trauma it creates a situation that is easily buried and hidden away. Children are taught to not talk about family "secrets". It is one of those subjects that are not welcome at the dinner table or at most family reunions.

Most people never face those demons and keep the skeletons buried deep inside. It might be fear, denial or some other coping mechanism that keeps us from coming to terms with our past. It might also be that we do not know how to heal the hurt. We continue through life believing that if we never think about the past, it will just go away; if we bury the hurtful memories deep enough, they will just disappear.

However, the truth is that if we do not deal with the hurt, it will just fester and grow like an open wound causing us to repeat mistakes over and over. How do I know this? I grew up surrounded by trauma. I have been working with Dale all of my adult life to heal the effects of living through family trauma. Together, we have healed much hurt and pain by using many of the tools discussed in her writings. Healing is a process which sometimes takes daily work.

Dale and I have a history together, as I am the little sister, referred to as "It" in the book. Today, I can honestly say: "I forgive you." It has taken a lifetime for me to forgive. Trauma has an emotional impact on all parts of your life. This book will help provide therapeutic tools for positive change.

V. (a.k.a. "Sue")

Preface Two: From my daughter

Each of us is born into a culture, a family, or a world that aims to create a sense of safety or belonging. Often the first word that a baby learns is the word, "mamma". We use that word to describe the one that feeds us, that rocks us to sleep, or the one that creates our first concept of the term "home". Whether home becomes a safe place or not ... it is something that we learn to trust EXISTS. It is where you go when you have nowhere else to go. It is the net that catches you when you have nowhere else to fall.

As we grow into ourselves and redefine ourselves we often go through periods where we reject our "mother". We deny our culture. We run away from home. We fight against the patterns that be and the powers that have worked to define who we think we are. We break free from constrictions and build our own identity. This is a natural process ... and often it can feel incredibly traumatic. As we grow into adolescence and adulthood we gain perspective on the patterns that have led us to the way we define our world and the way we define ourselves.

We no longer need to feel constricted by the views and norms of the past. We no longer need to feel constricted by the patterns that we have assumed to be "the way things are." We don't need to be the person that our parents dreamed we would become. Or we can find the power to create dreams of our own if we believe that our parents never had the strength, power, or time to create dreams for us.

We have the power to define who we are and who we want to be. We have the power to change the patterns that have misled us into feeling a false sense of "normalcy" or "safety". Just because we have learned to accept that things exist in a certain way in our lives, our families, our cultures, and our society ... doesn't mean that we don't have the power to challenge those norms and find a new, refreshing, empowering way of living our lives.

Everyone has a mother. Everyone has experienced trauma in one form or another. Whether it was that look that your mother gave you that made you feel unloved, or if you had a dream of becoming someone or doing something that existed outside of the expectations put on you by family or society. You have the power to change the pattern.

This book is a gift. It tells the story of a woman who is willing to share the pain she experienced and the trauma she lived as a result of having parents that repeated the patterns of the past. Dale Bach tells her story with grace and with the perspective of a person that has invested in a lifetime of healing. She shares heart wrenching stories of childhood trauma, experiences you wouldn't wish upon your worst enemy, so that you can have faith and trust that transformation is possible. You have the power to change. She is proof that if you can choose to break patterns of abuse and self-destruction to become a better version of your true self, and create new patterns of healing, love, and nurturing.

I know this best, because I am her daughter.

Ingrid Siss
Kindergarten teacher

MAMMA TRAUMA

CONTENTS

1: STARTING YOUR JOURNEY

Let us begin with the good news. Everyone has a mom.
And everyone has mother issues. You might not think of that
as good news, but in fact, it is. You've got plenty of company...
and you've got a way forward. These issues often arise when
we begin new friendships, relationships, start new projects, or
even begin new careers. Sometimes we find ourselves
repeating patterns that no longer serve us. We ask ourselves,
how did I get here ... again?

The first step to healing from Mamma Trauma is
recognizing there are issues. This is where we will begin our
journey. Throughout this book I will present you with
different healing modalities so that you can identify your
issues and heal from painful experiences from your past. You
can gain hope, reclaim your freedom and awaken your joy.
Now is a time for change. If you are ready and willing, this
book will give you tools to guide that change, and serve as a
reminder that you are not alone. You are never alone. The bad
news? This work is not easy. It takes time, energy and
courage. But you already knew that, didn't you?

I believe nothing is an accident. You are, right now,
exactly where you are meant to be. And because you are ready

for what follows in these pages, you are ready for your first and maybe your most important lesson: You are precisely where you are supposed to be at this very moment, and you are being taken care of by something that is greater than yourself; whether you choose to call this Source, Higher Power, Spirit, God, Allah, Buddha, Divine Intelligence, Tao, or Nature. This is what you are supposed to do next, because here you are doing it. Your job is simply to trust that you will receive the guidance, the tools, the protection, and the care you need. Throughout this book, I will use different names to refer to the Divine, but please use the name that works best for you.

At one point in my life, when I was at a low point, I asked for and received a mantra that could get me through the storms I was facing in my life. Here are the words I received: *God takes care of the sparrow ... God will take care of me.*

> *"You may have struggled and experienced pain in the past, but those struggles and that pain happened for a reason: To strengthen you."*

Any time I got scared, I would say that to myself. Those words were exactly the ones I needed. They always remind me of who is taking care of me! Every time I see a sparrow, I am reminded that my first job is to trust.

By the way, if you don't believe in or trust in God, Nature will work just as well for whatever your mantra turns out to be. Go spend a morning or an afternoon looking at and experiencing the ocean, the trees, the flowers, or the sky. I do

2

all of that as often as I can. Spend some time with Nature, and you will realize before too long that it is Nature that nurtures you and all other living things. This realization leads us to powerful mantras:

If a giant oak tree grows from that little acorn,
what am I to grow into?

If a delicate wild flower can grow strong and beautiful
between the cracks of a busy city sidewalk,
then I can grow strong, too!

If God is the ocean, I am the wave. We are One.

Believe it or not, there is still time, as you read these words, for Nature to do its job ... which is to help you reclaim your freedom.

I know this because (as you will learn in the chapters that follow) I've experienced all kinds of trauma, pain, and abuse in my own life, and I've now reached a point of joy. I've moved beyond being a victim to being a victor ... by reclaiming my own power, tapping into a source of timeless wisdom and intelligence, and harnessing the massive leverage of forgiveness in my life. I wrote this book because I have a mission to fulfill. I want to help everyone I possibly can learn to use the same force, forgiveness, and to reach the same place of power and joy.

3

Of course, I realize that depending on where you are in your life, "forgiveness" may be a huge word to lift at the moment; a word that may sound too much like "defeat", a word you may not quite be ready for yet. That's all right. Think of me as your guide. I am here to help you build up your innate emotional and spiritual strength. Together, we can work our way up to the true meaning of the word "forgiveness", which is much closer to "freedom" and "victory" than it is to "surrender."

There is time for all that. What is important for us to understand now is that, as difficult and painful as our past experiences may have been for us, there really is a process we can use to free ourselves, a process that will allow us travel through those experiences safely and reach the other side, where we will discover a more profound sense of peace and boundless joy. At the end of each chapter, you will find a "healing modality." These are direct ways for you to take back your power and change destructive patterns in your life.

The process is all about finding peace – between your mom and yourself, of course, but between you and everyone else as well. That's my intention for you here, my bottom line for all who encounter these words: absolute freedom, peace, and joy. The sooner we begin this journey, the sooner you can experience deep compassion, deep understanding, and deep love in your own life, become a more beneficial presence to yourself and others, and stop sleepwalking through your precious time on this earth. You may have struggled and experienced pain in the past, but those struggles and that pain happened for a reason: To strengthen you.

Once upon a time, a man saw a brand-new butterfly in the final stages of struggle, desperate to shed its cocoon. It seemed to be working so hard, and making progress so slowly, that he reached for his pocketknife, and prepared to gently open that cocoon so the newborn butterfly could escape. But before he did anything, he thought twice, kneeled in prayer, and asked God for help and guidance ... and an angel descended and said, "You may cut open the cocoon if you wish, but if you do, the butterfly will spend its whole life misshapen and incapable of flight. When it emerges, it will be waterlogged for a lifetime, and its wings will be too weak to lift it into the air. If you leave it alone to struggle for a time, however, it will shed its weakness and be ready to fly when it emerges. The striving has a purpose; you will do the butterfly the greatest good by letting it emerge on its own."

From our past struggles comes our current strength.

"Walk in the power and strength of Love.
Therein is Peace, Joy & Freedom."

~~~~~~~~~~~~~

HEALING MODALITY: CENTERING YOURSELF

Healing begins with the decision to center yourself. To center yourself, you need to connect your breath to the center of your heart. Take in a deep breath as if you are breathing into the center of your heart with the intention of connecting to Divinity (to something bigger than yourself). As you do this, feel or imagine that the center of your chest is filled with golden light. Hold your breath with that intention for three seconds, then as you slowly release all the air in your lungs through your mouth, let go of every thought and feeling that separates you from your Divinity. After you exhale, hold your breath at the very end for another three seconds.

On your next breath, breathe in as if through the center of your chest. Imagine you are breathing in light, feeling love and peace. Hold that for a moment and feel the light in every cell of your body. When you release your breath, imagine that you are breathing out all stress with the intention of sending it to the very center of the earth. Continue the process. Breathe in light. Breathe out anything that would block the light. Center yourself inside the center of your heart space with the intention of connecting to your Higher Power, to God, to Divine Intelligence, or whatever word you use for Divinity; connect to that now.

From this place of connection, know that there is only One Power. Like the wave is connected to the ocean, you are connected to this divine power. Open up and allow yourself to receive this, sensing and knowing your oneness. Let the Divine Light of the universe fill your mind your heart and every cell of your body, right now.

PRAYER FOR CENTERING

Note: the parts in [brackets] are the parts I encourage you to rephrase as you see fit.

[Source of All that Is, Heavenly Father. Divine Mother. Holy Spirit, legions of angels connected to the Highest Source of Love and Light.]

I now surrender to you, anything and everything that has kept me separate from realizing my Oneness with you. I open up and ask to be guided by you and to be shown clearly the way that is for my highest good. I surrender all fears, all pain of the past, all judgments, all blame. I give it to you. I don't want it anymore. I empty myself now and am filled with the divine light, love and wisdom of my true authentic self. It is from this place of Oneness that I claim and know that I am a divine emanation of the Most High.

That peace that passes human understanding is my birthright. Beauty is my divine essence. Joy is the truth of my soul. I connect to this and I allow myself to be set free knowing this truth. Please guide me and allow me to heal those places inside of myself that still hurt.

Please elevate my perception so I may really be able to see the truth that will set me free. Help me go beyond blame and shame so that I may find my wholeness once again.

8

Thank you for this. My heart is filled with gratitude. I know that it is already done and I say, "YES!" with every part of my body, mind and soul. I release this word to the law of manifestation. I know it is so. And it is done. So be it. It is done. Amen and so it is.

2: FROM PUNISHING SELF TO SELF LOVE

One day, about 22 years ago, I learned that my housekeeper kept important information from me about my daughters, information that I needed to have. When I confronted her about this, and asked her why she had kept the information from me, she said something bizarre: She hated telling me things that would upset me.

"Why is that?" I asked.

She told me that it scared her to watch me beat my thighs with my fists in anger and frustration, which was what I did when she shared bad news with me.

> *"To begin healing I needed to trust myself. I needed to trust that I was capable of healing. It takes courage to trust."*

I was totally unaware that I did this to myself. I almost didn't believe her ... until I remembered the times when I found myself wondering where and how I had gotten those nasty bruises on my thighs. I just assumed I must have been bumping into things a lot.

This exchange with my housekeeper was when I realized that I needed some real help. It was the trigger event that led me to find a therapist who taught me about self-talk. My first assignment was to sing a little song he sang for me: "I love myself the way I am, there's nothing I need to change." (Louise Hay made that a famous healing song in the 1980s.)

Whenever I started to sing the song, I would break down and cry. I just couldn't get the words out without sobbing. After many months of practice, I was finally able to sing it little by little, but it took me over a year with diligent practice to get the whole song out without sobbing. That was one of my first breakthroughs. It all came from the realization that there was a problem and then choosing to make a commitment to identify what it was so I could begin the work of healing myself. To begin healing I needed to trust myself. I needed to trust that I was capable of healing. It takes courage to trust.

PRAYER OF DISCOVERY

Great Oneness, Divine Intelligence, I know that I am one with the power of Love which is stronger than any other power in the universe. I surrender all fear, doubt, trepidations to the power of Love and Light. I ask from the deepest part of my being for divine guidance, clarity and courage to look and find the patterns that have been destructive in my life. I am ready, willing and able to take the action of self-inquiry. I am choosing to go into my past to find the saboteurs and patterns that have kept me small, constricted, in pain, and in emotional bondage. I ask for the help of my Higher Self and

Inner Counselor to assist me with this. I thank you for this and as I release this word to the Law, I know it is done. Thank you, and so it is.

~~~~~~~~~~~~

HEALING MODALITY: IDENTIFY YOUR ISSUES

I hit obstacles all the time. I'm sure you do, too. What I
have learned over time is I can't avoid obstacles but I can
identify the obstacle more accurately whenever I run into one.
If it is self-created I find ways to understand the cause of the
problem and recognize what my part was in creating the
obstacle. I forgive myself and seek out the lesson learned. I
find the gift, I reframe it, I let it go, and I move on. I paint a
new picture of what I want in its place. Usually, this is the
opposite of the obstacle I just encountered. This process takes
courage.

Trust is the foundation of courage. How do you build
trust? When you hit an obstacle, you name it, you claim it, and
you ask, "What is the positive benefit from it?" This is what
makes true courage possible.

Don't mistake courage for never being scared. Courage is
identifying what really happened ... and then finding a way to
move forward intelligently.

Therapy taught me that I needed courage to move beyond
self-hatred. That was what caused all the "accidents" that I had
had in my life: I believed I had a need for punishment when
others didn't punish me. I would find ways to hurt myself. This
problem was not the result of a single incident, but came from
many parts of my experience. It was like a virus that my
computer sucked up somewhere.

The great lesson of my life is this: The only way I can resolve a problem or change it when it happens is by first identifying what it is.

This healing modality takes 10 to 20 minutes. Please find an uninterrupted place and time to be by yourself. Have a piece of paper and pen with you. Sit down and take three long, slow breaths to become very present in the moment.

Imagine with the first breath that you are breathing in light. Hold your breath for three seconds, and let out anything and everything of the past that is blocking you. Exhale fully and completely. At the end of your breath, hold for three seconds and then breathe in fully. Breathe in more love and light. Hold it for three seconds and then breathe out any and all thoughts and feelings of the past. Right now, you are getting present. Hold the breath at the end for three seconds, and then breathe in the present moment. Hold it for three seconds and breathe out all future ideas, worries or concerns. Now breathe in the present moment. Breathe out and naturally allow yourself to become very still. Good.

Now, take a deep breath, hold it for three seconds and think about your mother. When you think about her, let your breath out and become aware of what you're feeling in your body. Is there any tension in your arms, your legs, your heart or your stomach? Notice now in the next few moments as you think about your mother; think about when you were a little girl or little boy and see if any pictures come to your mind. See if there is an issue of hurt feelings, pain or not feeling good about yourself in your inner being. Write down on the paper what those issues might be.

Some examples could be: "I don't deserve love, success, to be happy." "I can never do anything right." "I'm selfish." "Nothing works out for me." "I'll never be good enough." "I'm a bad boy" or "I'm a bad girl" and "I deserve to be punished." "My Mamma doesn't really love me or care about me." "I'm not lovable." "I was a mistake" and "My parents are too busy for me." "I am not wanted." "I am not worthy of love."

Did you ever have a parent say something like "I wish you had never been born?" Or "My life would have been so much easier without you?" If so, you might just have some issues to resolve. To survive deep childhood pain, we push these issues down in our bodies and do our best to forget about them. Unfortunately, they tend to pop up later in life and make having a loving, healthy life and balanced relationships hard, if not impossible. In fact, they act like little saboteurs.

Look at your life and remember when you had the promise of really being loved or loving someone. Now look and see if there are any patterns that show up. Did you feel unloved, uncared for or rejected? This exercise is not an excuse to wallow in the past, but a tool to help you identify issues that come up over and over again in your life. Issues that come up might be abandonment, unworthiness, or needing to be punished.

Once you identify your issues, you are well on your way to recovering from your own personal experience of the universal phenomenon I call "Mamma Trauma".

3:   WHERE I CAME FROM

This is not an autobiography, but in order to benefit from all I have learned and experienced about Mamma Trauma, you will need to know some things about me. Some of it is easy to read (and write) and some of it is hard. I'll begin with the easy part in this chapter.

I was born to a blended family in Flushing, New York in 1949. My dad, Harry, came from an upper-middle-class family in College Point, New York and was known as Wild Harry. He was, I am told, a speakeasy frequenter who danced the Charleston, ate raw goldfish, and played ice hockey on a motorcycle. He loved boating and enjoyed living life to its fullest. He was debonair, charismatic and very handsome. He had just lost his wife, and was working as a New York City fireman when he met my mother, Kitty, in a bar. At the time, Dad was looking for a wife ... and also looking for a mother for his young son and daughter at home.

Kitty had tried and failed to make it as a singer. She was feisty, fiery, independent, intelligent, and radiantly beautiful; she had been named Miss Newark of 1938. She had been invited to go on to compete for the Miss America title, but her overprotective Italian father had vetoed that idea. I always heard sadness in her voice when she spoke of that part of her life.

Kitty had grown up in a lower-middle-class family, and grew up during a time when it was hard to be lower middle-class in America. She told me tales of standing in soup lines during the Great Depression. Her father was a house painter, and her mother was infamous, both for her affairs and for being as cold as ice. Perhaps not surprisingly, considering the role model my grandmother provided, my mom's own marital history did not get off to a good start.

Mamma

The first time around, my mother married a man who was in the service. He was away on duty when she met my dad. She had a two-year-old son. And she fell for my dad anyway.

I can only imagine that she was lonely and seeking connection.

From what I can gather, there was very little love in that first marriage. My mother had married a man who appeared to have some money because she wanted to better her economic situation. He had married her because she was beautiful. But they were not happy.

Kitty and Harry fell deeply in love the night they met in that bar. Kitty quickly filed for divorce, and within ten months they were married. They were known as the lovebirds of the family. They lived a long and full life together, and as Dad would say, they "lived high off the hog" despite my dad's several career changes. They always maintained a sense of great gratitude for their life together.

Much of what follows is about my relationship with my mother. It has taken me a long time to get to a point in my life where I could tell any part of my mother's life story with compassion. My intention here is to share my story, which intersects with hers, in the hope that it may awaken and heal the enormous pain that so many mothers share with their children. I will be sharing the experience of my own wounding in that relationship for a specific purpose: to share and help you learn from the lessons and the healing that followed.

"I will be sharing the experience of my own wounding ... for a specific purpose: to share and help you learn from the lessons and the healing that followed."

~~~~~~~~~~~~

HEALING EXERCISE: MIRROR WORK

Did you complete the healing modalities in chapters one and two? If not, you will want to go back and complete them now. If so ... let's keep going.

I assume that you have found a couple issues that you might want to work on. I suggest you work on only one issue at a time. Determine which issue has the biggest hold on you. Guess what? This is going to be the one that gives you the most discomfort when you think about it. This is what you need to address first.

Find a time when you will be uninterrupted and you can be alone for at least twenty to thirty minutes. Unplug yourself from the world. Turn off your cell phone. This is a time for you to go within yourself to see where you are. Go to a mirror. Look at yourself and see who you are. Look into your eyes. Look at your face and, if you can, your body as well. (Note: When you make the statements that you're about to read, I want you to write down what your mind says back to you. This is to identify the self-talk that has been going on inside your head. This will also help you identify the patterns that are controlling your life.)

Say the following words and notice where you feel pain or discomfort in your body:

"I love myself just the way I am."

Was it easy or difficult to say? Did you feel good about what you said? Did it hurt? Was it hard to say? Did you feel that you were lying to yourself?

Next, insert your name:

"I love you, _____, just as you are."

Again: How did you feel as you said this? Was it easy or difficult to say?

Next, focus on your body. Look at your face. Look at your skin. Look into your eyes and say:

"I love you. You are a precious, beautiful being and I am so glad that I get to be connected to you."

Now, all this may seem a little crazy, but just put aside all the crazy thoughts and feelings that will rise up during this exercise. Be persistent no matter how silly you feel. Be sure to make an effort to say all of the following before you move on to the next chapter:

"I love you, _____, just the way you are."

**"I am worthy of the best that love
and life have to offer."**

"I am beautiful and I love the way I look."

"I love who I am and I love how other people treat me."

"I love the way I treat other people."

"I didn't deserve what my Mamma (or Poppa) did to me."

"I never deserved to be treated like that."
(When you say these last two things, notice how you feel in your body, in your heart and what thoughts are racing in your mind. This is an exercise in self-knowing.)

Now look into your eyes and say:

"No matter what happened to me, I am strong. Even though I may have been hurt in my past, there is a gift here. There is a blessing. I may not know what it is now, but I am willing and ready to commit to finding out the blessings. I am ready to heal. I am ready to be committed to my healing. I am willing to do what it takes."

MAKE A CONTRACT WITH YOURSELF

I, _____ (your name)
on _____ (the date) am ready, willing
and capable of making a commitment to my healing and my
recovery from my past trauma. I know there are gifts here and
I am choosing to do what it takes to heal and to find those gifts
that come from the healing process.

_____
(your signature)

And so it is.

4: SUFFERING IN SILENCE

I am now a grown woman, looking back on a life that has had its share of trauma, and considering carefully the various choices and conclusions I made at the time in response to that trauma. I am celebrating new and better choices and conclusions I'm making along the way whenever I can. I'm dealing with my issues, just as you're dealing with yours. The first big issue I can remember having to deal with in my own life was something I call "Suffering in Silence." Here is my first memory of it.

Long before my sister was born, there was a beautiful summer evening when I had Mamma and Daddy all to myself. We were out on a drive together, the three of us. The windows were down, and the cool breeze was carrying us gently through the heat of the highway. We were going somewhere that required nice clothes.

I was sitting in the back, all dressed up; Mamma and Daddy were in the front, talking and laughing. I felt such love from them. They really did love each other a lot, and I was caught up in that love and carried away by it.

Out of a three-year-olds curiosity, I decided to explore a strange button that was set into the door, right by my left arm.

I pushed the button down. A moment later, it magically popped back up. I pulled it out. On the end was a bright orange glow. I wanted to touch its beautiful glow, to see how it felt. I put my little finger on that bright glowing round circle.

It was (I know now) the cigarette lighter. It hurt so badly that I felt like screaming, but I did not want to interrupt my mother and father, didn't want to spoil the beautiful moment. So I sat there with my finger blistering, with tears rolling down my cheeks crying as quietly as humanly possible. My pain did not matter. I was not worth being comforted. So I suffered in silence.

I can't begin to count how many times this pattern played out. Later, when I was seven, I would make drinks for my parents, like scotch on the rocks. They would smile wide as they smoked their cigarettes and drank their cocktails. But I never joined in their conversation. After all, children were meant to be seen, not heard. They were busy with their life, and it seemed as if I was an interruption to their fun, a burden, unwanted. I made them their drinks and wished I could be part of their smiling and talking. Again, I suffered in silence.

When I was in elementary school, Mom would leave twelve cents on the kitchen table for me to buy my breakfast on my way to school. She would say, "Get a carton of milk and a pastry." In those days it cost five cents for milk and seven cents for a pastry. Instead, I got a soda pop and a sugar glazed doughnut. This was my daily breakfast.

After school I would walk through empty lots and collect bottles. I would take them to the store and get two cents a bottle and buy as many chocolate bars as I could afford I would eat every one of them, and then I would pass out. I'd wake up feeling groggy and even more depressed. No wonder I had trouble concentrating at school!

I continued this pattern of soda pop and sugary doughnuts for breakfast from second grade until I graduated from high school. This unhealthy habit set up my pattern of alcohol abuse, drug abuse, sex addiction, eating disorders, and—you guessed it – sugar addiction. It took me years of patient self-examination – and a lot of time with a lot of therapists – to come to terms with all of this.

But, I have to say; the biggest help of all is to meditate.

ONE OF THE BUILDING BLOCKS OF HEALING IS TO MEDITATE DAILY!

~~~~~~~~~~~~~

HEALING MODALITY: Bedtime Meditation

If you have unresolved issues that are keeping you awake
at night or giving you restless sleep, practicing bedtime
meditation can make a difference.

When you prepare to go to sleep, take 5 to 20 minutes for
your bedtime meditation. Begin by doing the centering
exercise (see Chapter One) to connect to your own Divinity.
Then, when you are completely relaxed, simply focus on
whatever question you have and ask to receive a clear answer
in the morning when you wake up – one that you will
understand, one that will resonate in your heart. Remember
that the quality of your life depends on the quality of the
questions you ask.

If you don't get a clear answer, don't give up ... ask every
night until you get an answer and make sure that you ask from
your heart. That means you have a burning desire to know the
answer. Don't ask unless you are willing to really feel the
answer in your heart ... and then follow the guidance you
receive.

Do not ask from a half-hearted place or from a place of
mere curiosity. You must come from a place of deep respect for
your Inner Guidance. Ask for courage to be clear enough, to
see and feel it, and then ask that the Highest and Best be
expressed in and through you.

Your assignment for tonight is to meditate for between
five and twenty minutes. Ask your guides and angels to work

with you in your sleep. Pick one aspect of your life where you need clarity or an answer, whether it is for self-expression, career, relationship, health, or finances; or you can merge two issues, like career and finances.

While in bed, take a deep breath, hold it briefly, and then let it out slowly. Do this three times or until you feel relaxed.

Connect with the deepest, sincerest part of your heart and soul, your own divinity. After you connect, you then ask your question. If you want, you can write your question on a piece of paper and put it under your pillow.

For example, ask, "What do I need to do to balance my body, mind, and spirit?" Or "What is the highest and best for me to do next in my life regarding creative expression and finances?" When you ask from a deep place and really want to know, you will get the answer. This develops trust and patience, which are qualities needed for your journey to recovery.

Example: What needs to happen in order for me to be clear on having a purpose-filled, purpose-driven, joy-filled life where I get to share all of my gifts and be of service and do what I have come to do? What might that look like?

- Ask with strong intention – what does that look like?

- Ask what you have to let go of in order to receive this with grace and ease.

- Ask for a clearer picture, sensation, words or dream that will help you understand.

- Ask what is your highest and best creative expression.

- Ask that it be connected to your divine purpose and that it brings you joy, peace, freedom, and abundance.

And then go to bed like a child on Christmas Eve and expect the answer to be there and trust. As you drift off into sleep, imagine waking up and having the answer. Feel your heart fill with deep and profound gratitude that you now have clarity.

Go to sleep counting the many blessings that you already have. And continue to feel and muster up more feeling of great appreciation.

The answer will come to you. TRUST!

5:   THE LEGACY OF THE BROOM

Once, during the last few years of her life, I asked my mother, "Did you ever feel loved by your mother? Did you ever feel any kind of connection with her?"

"No," she said, "I never did."

She had answered me so automatically, and with such unsettling calm, that I felt sure there just had to be more to the story. "Mom," I said, "There must be at least one time that you had some kind of loving connection with her. Please tell me about that."

She thought for a moment; a blank kind of look played across her face, a look that made me feel strange. "I remember the broom," she said. "My mother would come after me with the broom. I would hide under the bed until my father came home from work. When he did, I knew it was safe enough to come out."

That was it. No matter how I pressed, or what angle I used to approach the question from that day forward, the only memory I could get out of my mom about her own connection to her mother was of her cowering under a bed to avoid being hit by a broom.

That broom was my grandmother's legacy, because it was also part of my own relationship with my mother. Just as she cowered from my grandmother's brutality, I cowered from my mother's.

I remember being in the kitchen. I was about 11 years old, and I was busy teasing *it*, which was something I did on a frequent basis. "*It*" was how I referred to, and thought of, my sister, Sue, back then. From my perspective, *it* was not a person. *It* took all the attention away from me and I didn't like that. I

"When I first realized this generational pattern of abuse, I was a long way away from feeling any kind of solidarity with my mother."

teased *it* by poking *it* in the ribs, pulling *its* hair, or slipping my foot in front of *it*, laughing as *it* would fall. I didn't call *it* names; I would just get back at *it* by causing *it* physical pain and then laughing at *it*. I was the star and *it* was my co-star. *It* was my personal slapstick machine.

A side note: What I did to my sister years ago has caused me a lot of shame. It was buried deep and all but lost in my memory. As I remembered this, and wrote about it, the pain welled up yet again to be healed. Thankfully, my sister Sue has forgiven me. I have done a lot of inner child work to help little Dale heal and to forgive myself.

I was terrorizing *it* in the kitchen. My mother was also in the kitchen with her back turned to us. When she heard *it* fall and scream, she turned around, glared at me, grabbed a broom, and went after me. She raised the broom high in the air and then hit me – hard – with the filthy, prickly bristles. It hurt like hell, and it horrified me! I knew there were dead spiders and their cobwebs in those bristles, and now those disgusting things were on me.

She kept hitting me with that broom. Over and over again: on my stomach, my back, my arms, my legs, my head, anything she could reach. That was the first of many times she assaulted me with that broom. Of course, in one sense, she did not use the same physical broom every time she hit me.

But as an adult, I realized that the "broom" was the same weapon she had been hiding from when she, as a little girl, scrambled under the bed to hide from her mother. When I first realized this generational pattern of abuse, I was a long way away from feeling any kind of solidarity with my mother. The good news is that I broke the pattern and never hit my children with a broom—or anything else.

As I drew myself into a little ball on the kitchen floor in an attempt to disappear completely, I was busy making the decision, with feeling, that I was a bad girl who deserved this kind of punishment.

My experience with violence, starting at this early age, set up subconscious patterns that continued long after the assault; in the form of pain and suffering that I endured throughout my adult life.

How? The experts say that the subconscious mind directs about 85- 95% of our life. That was certainly true for me. If others did not play the role of victimizer, I would hurt myself through accidents, or by engaging in self-sabotaging behavior, or by behaving in a way that would bring out the worst in others and fulfill my role as a victim.

Many decades later, I give thanks for the emotional and mental balance that I am finally able to experience on a day-to-day basis. How do I know this? I am at peace. Even though situations and circumstances in my life are not exactly the way I want them, I am experiencing more peace, joy, love and laughter than I ever thought possible. I find myself surrendering to what is in the moment with great appreciation. And you can find peace, too.

HEALING MODALITY: HEALING YOUR INNER CHILD

I learned in my Master's program of Spiritual Psychology at the University of Santa Monica, that the definition of healing was finding where you hurt and pouring unconditional love into the pain. I have witnessed that when your inner child has not been healed, it acts as a saboteur to get attention, to protect you and keep you safe ... because it wants to be your ally not your enemy.

Doing this exercise requires that you trust your first impulse and allow yourself to go along with it. Imagination is a very important part of your subconscious mind. In fact, this is a powerful way for you to tap into your imagination. You have an inner child that lives within your subconscious and within your heart chakra. Your heart chakra is simply an energy center that is in the center of your chest where your feelings reside. Ask your Inner Counselor (or your Higher Self) to help you connect to your inner child with the intention of giving voice to a younger part of yourself so that healing may take place.

Please allow yourself at least 20 minutes to an hour for this exercise. Make sure you have no interruptions, unplug the phone and give yourself the gift of alone time for healing. Set up your sacred space by lighting a candle. Then sit in a comfortable chair with both feet on the floor, legs uncrossed, with back straight and sit back on your sit bones. You will need to keep your spine straight to allow yourself the support to breathe deeply and keep your energy free flowing. You will need to keep your feet on the floor for grounding.

Connect to your Higher Power through intention. As you are breathing in, imagine that you are breathing in through the center of your chest, filling your whole body with light. Hold your breath for three seconds. As you breathe out, imagine that you are breathing out through your chest, with the intention of releasing any and all stress, worries, and fears.

On your second breath, breathe in as if you are breathing in the present moment through the center of your chest. Hold your breath for three seconds. Now release your breath slowly, deeply and completely, as if all your thoughts of everything from your past are expelled through the center of your chest. Breathe into the center of your chest imagining every cell of your body is filled with golden light, becoming fully present, calling your spirit back from the past and the future. Hold this beautiful picture in your mind and heart for three seconds while your lungs are full and then slowly and completely release this loving light throughout your whole body. Then resume your natural breathing and ask your Higher Power and your Inner Counselor to help you reveal exactly what needs to be healed. Allow the deepest healing possible with grace and ease.

Close your eyes after connecting to your own divinity. Ask for your inner child to appear. Go within yourself and see this little one. How old is your inner child? One? Three? Five? Seven? Ask your inner child to talk to you.

You may start the conversation by saying something like this: "Hey, little (your name), I know it might have been a long time since we've connected, but I would like to connect with you now. Is there anything that I can give you? Are you willing to talk with me?" When you get a response be very loving, gentle and kind. Treat your little one like she/he is the most precious little child in the entire universe. Allow yourself to really feel love and compassion for this little one that might have been neglected, hurt physically, mentally or emotionally. This is your time to re-parent the little child inside of you.

When I was doing inner work, the first time I contacted my inner child she was dressed in camouflage clothes, matted hair and had knives and machine guns. She was very angry and very unhappy with me. It took me many months of going inside myself before she would talk to me. Her name was Rambo. I kept telling her that I loved her and I felt sorry for the pain that she had to endure. I promised her I would never let anybody hurt her again. I would protect her and keep her safe.

Slowly she began to trust me. She would say to me, "Let's go for an ice cream!" I would close my eyes and imagine that we went to the best ice cream store and ate the ice cream together. That was the beginning of healing my inner child.

When your little one tells you what she/he wants, imagine it and go for it! Working with your inner child and your subconscious mind is a highly rewarding experience and a very powerful healing tool.

I suggest that you check in with your inner child once a day for 30 days. Put the appointment on your calendar so you will remember. Once you get the hang of connecting with your inner child on a daily basis, it might only take three to five minutes per day. You will receive a large return on a very small time investment. Your inner child will give you energy, vitality and joy.

Start a journal to document how you feel when you begin this exercise ... and how you feel after the 30 days. Have fun with your inner child! Many times you will begin to feel more energy and happiness for no apparent reason.

6: MOMMY MONSTER

I stayed silent, close to the door, and tried to make myself invisible as I watched my mother beat my brother with a belt.

I was six years old. He was thirteen. And she was brutalizing him. The belt buckle would hit his skin, and he would scream, "Stop, please stop!" The smacking sound of the leather on my brother's skin made my knees buckle and made me shiver to the bone.

My mother seemed like a madwoman to me, like someone from the movies, like a monster had somehow jumped inside my mother's body. Mommy Monster! I started to laugh hysterically, which really confused me. I didn't think any of this was funny, but I was so scared and horror-stricken that this crazy laughter came out of me of its own volition. (I now know that this is a common response to traumatic stress.)

My brother heard me, glared at me, and immediately became angry with me. He thought I was laughing at him. I think he made the decision, at that moment in his life, that he hated me.

I remember the long silence after I laughed. I remember that the air by the doorway was thick. I remember running away from that archway where I had seen my mother beat my brother with the belt. I felt helpless. I remember wanting to die. Why? Because I had just witnessed something that happened to my brother, and I felt like it had happened to me, except worse. I had discovered myself laughing, and it wasn't funny. Even at that age, I knew that was a horrible thing for me to watch. That image has stayed with me all my life.

Do not judge people by what they laugh at. Perhaps their mind is playing tricks on them, like my mind did back then. After that day, my brother, George, was never nice to me again – not, at least, until I was an adult. For a child, it certainly felt like forever.

~~~~~~~~~~~~

HEALING MODALITY: Prayer Changes the Conditioned Mind

Prayer is focused thought merging the heart to the Divine Mind. We use prayer to embody the cellular memory of joy and radiate the presence of Peace, Love, and Light. This is a prayer for connecting to Divine Mother first thing in the morning.

HEALING PRAYER: THE PATH TO WHOLENESS

Divine Mother, hold me in your heart today. I open my heart so your unconditional love may flow through you to me, from heaven to earth. Let me be gentle as I walk through this day. Let me be the love I so deeply crave so that I may bring beauty everywhere I go with my presence. Let me make time for myself to be touched by nature and allow my sensuality to open like a flower in the sunshine. Let the sweet perfume of my soul essence sweeten the air as the vibration is transformed from fear to love in moments of self-remembering.

Pivot my old thoughts of reacting from my conditioned mind to this moment of my awakened heart-mind. Awaken and open my heart to the soft whispering of love's soul song. Let me truly hear the birds as they greet life with joy.

Let my tears from letting go of the illusions purify my soul so that my light may be seen and brighten this world. Remind me to be grateful for all of the good that has graced me.

41

Please release me from the judgments that I have placed on myself and on others. These attachments feel like barnacles on my sailing vessel, they slow me down and eat the body of my soul.

I release all of my separateness to you as I walk through this path of beauty today with you, shining your love and light through my heart. I know I am one with true beauty today as we leave flowers where our footsteps have been.

Thank you, thank you, thank you! And so it is, Amen.

7: SLAPPING IS CONTAGIOUS

I don't remember exactly how old I was the very first time I was slapped in the face, but I have figured out that it must have been around the time when I was five, but I was not yet in kindergarten. I do remember that it happened in public, and that it was my mother who slapped me.

I was being persistent about something or other that I wanted, the way any bright, talkative young child would be when being led through a store that contains exactly what she wants. To this day, I cannot recall what I was pestering my mother for. All I remember is that I wanted something and I kept asking her for it, and when I wouldn't stop, she pulled her arm back and slapped me – hard!

The pain I felt on my face when she slapped me was almost as bad as the emotional shock that ran through my whole body. That shock was deeper, broader, and wider than any physical pain could possibly have been. It was the deep sensation of betrayal. I felt embarrassed, ashamed, and humiliated that my mother had slapped me in public, for no other reason than I had kept on asking her for something. I hadn't known that she would do that. She had lost patience, but I had lost something, too.

That was the moment I made a life decision: If I ask for what I want, I get punished.

It's hard to say exactly what it was that I had lost when I made that decision, but looking back I know it had something to do with dignity, something that even a child could tell needed to be restored somehow.

When I went home and looked in the mirror I saw puffy red welts on my face, in the shape of my mother's hand. The welts only lasted one day, but the emotional scars took decades to heal.

From this day forward, touching felt odd to me. The only touches I remember as a child were the painful ones.

> "The message I drew from that experience ... was that I get punished and humiliated when I persistently ask for what I want."

Later, when my mother and I went shopping, I told her I wanted her to buy me another toy – maybe it was a doll. Instead, she bought me a wooden paddle toy, the kind with a string and a red ball attached to it.

With a strange sound in her voice and a glint in her eye she said, "So you want a toy, do you? Here's a toy. When you are naughty, I can use this on you instead of my hand. I don't like hurting my hand when I hit you."

After a few days, the darn string broke. I tried to hide it but Mamma found it in time for my punishment. From then on the toy was Mamma's and it would hurt me more than it hurt Mamma.

The message I drew from that childhood experience, and the decision I made with feeling, was that I get punished and humiliated when I persistently ask for what I want.

Later, after I had entered school, I found myself watching a dramatic scene from an old Hollywood movie that was playing on TV. In this scene, a sexy, powerful woman felt insulted by what some man had said. She slapped his face and said, "How dare you!" That scene captured my imagination, and I thought about it all afternoon and all evening. Of course, it echoed the painful memories of my shopping trips with Mamma. And it got me thinking: This is how grown-ups make a point!

The next day, I was out walking to school with a sweet-natured little boy I had made friends with in first grade. I still remember his name. It was Hughie. I remember deciding that he would be perfect to practice on. Out of the blue, I said, "How dare you!" and slapped his little face as hard as I could. For a second, I felt extremely powerful.

Then he started to cry – which the man in the movie had not done – and as his tears streamed down his face, I felt horrible. "Why did you do that?" he sobbed.

All I could say was, "I just wanted to know how it felt." It seemed like no explanation at all. Now I hurt deep inside. I wished I had never hit him when I saw the pain I had caused him. That may well have been the first time in my life I felt compassion and remorse.

~~~~~~~~~~~~

HEALING MODALITY: Breaking the Victim Role

Did you know that watching a violent television show or movie can have a powerful impact on your nervous system? It can impact your body, mind, and spirit. Did you know that it jump-starts your adrenal glands and releases cortisol, a steroid hormone, which causes the "fight, flight or freeze" response in your body? When this response is activated and you do not run or fight, hormones back up into your body and create mental blocks, nervousness, undue stress, fatigue and cloudy thinking; this process is proven to lead to multiple diseases. There are many scientific studies that verify this.

When you watch the news, play a violent videogame, or do anything else that your mind perceives as a threat, your body reacts, and not in the most positive way. This response can also activate the victim role.

When we are in our victim role we give up having a full, happy, healthy life. When I watched the show and saw that the woman looked so sexy and powerful by slapping the man, it gave me a twisted perception of reality. I became a perpetrator of violence. I became the one with power, and Hughie became the victim. Often the victim becomes a perpetrator. They may not easily recognize their contributions to the drama because it is easier to blame instead of accept responsibility. This pattern is activated and sustains abusive relationships.

How do we recover from taking on a victim role? Our environment has a powerful influence. We always have a choice of what to feed our minds. We can find good books, rent good movies, listen to healing music, meditate, exercise or walk in nature. For at least one week, steer yourself away from negative media influences, and do something that is positive and uplifting, something that makes you feel good.

HEALING MODALITY: THE FEEL GOOD BAROMETER

Make yourself a feel good barometer, numbered from one to ten, with zero being "I feel horrible" and ten being "I feel on top of the world." Before you begin the week-long media-free diet I recommend above, use the barometer to chart where you are when you watch the news or read a book about serial killers, then chart where you are when you watch a comedy that makes you laugh, or listen to a concert that makes you feel alive and happy, or take a walk in nature.

For one week, as you change your habits, chart it on your Feel Good Barometer and see if you notice a difference in your thoughts and feelings. This practice will bring greater awareness to how your environment affects your state of being.

8: ON MAMMA'S LAP – NOT

Most people "just go through" and laugh about their sibling rivalry, but for others, it can still be very painful. By the time I was four, I was used to my Mom primping, grooming, and showing me off as her beautiful doll, her daughter. Then my world changed. My sister was born. I had been the star, had been getting all the attention, and had been feeling special, when my world came crashing down. I was demoted to big sister, something I never asked for. I could never imagine someone replacing me in my starring role as The Beautiful One.

I got pushed aside. From the corner that I was sent to on a regular basis (for being bad), I would watch my mother adore this little thing they called Sue. I was now cast in the role of the sad, angry child, and I was labeled selfish, mean and jealous. I was once loved, cherished and adored, but now I was ugly, bad, and no good. I thought my mother had forgotten that she loved me once. If there ever was a hell, I fell into it.

Whenever my younger sister Sue got on Mamma's lap, I felt that I never did anymore. That feeling was always difficult for me to deal with. There was one Christmas Eve in particular when I recall that I was feeling very, very lonely. Sue was around four-and-a-half years old at this point, with shoulder length, wavy, golden brown hair. Mamma was carefully brushing Sue's hair. I could sense the closeness and love that they had for each other. I could sense that it was a special time for them; something I couldn't share, something I couldn't have. I was nine years old.

Mamma never brushed my hair that way. My hair was all curly and frizzy. There were always tangles, and it would always hurt when she brushed my hair. She tried, but she could hardly manage to brush it at all, much less brush it with the kind of love and attention that she did Sue's.

That Christmas Eve, I saw that they had a special connection, a very strong bond around that ritual of hair brushing that anyone would have sensed, just by walking into the room. There was a real sense of oneness and love. Watching them have such sweet closeness made my own feelings of being separate and far away from Mamma hurt even more deeply inside.

> *"Watching them have such sweet closeness made my own feelings of being separate and far away from Mamma hurt even more deeply inside."*

I was watching this scene from the dark hallway, spying on them. Standing there silently, I can remember concluding that Sue was very lovable, and that there must have been something really wrong with me, because I just was not lovable. I decided that it must be because I was really ugly or something like that. I felt this horrible sensation start to grow inside my heart and in my solar plexus.

It felt like a black, empty, dull, throbbing, horrible pain. Very dark thoughts started to grow in my mind: Why should she get all the attention? Why was she even born? How come she has to be there on my Mamma's lap? Mamma loves her. Mamma doesn't love me anymore. Everything was fine before she came along. I hate her. I want her gone. I want her dead.

Maybe I can kill her.

~~~~~~~~~~~~

HEALING MODALITY: PRACTICE SELF-LOVE

Now that you are aware that you have issues and patterns that are painful, and now that you know that when you look in the mirror (see Chapter Three) it's hard to say, "I love you," it's easier to realize that you lack self-love.

What is self-love anyway? It's not narcissism. Self-love is simply saying and knowing that you are worthy and deserve all the good that Love and Life have to offer. You deserve and are worthy of having loving people around you.

Self-love should be the yardstick by which we measure our relationships and every situation we build for ourselves. Ask: Does being around this person make me feel expanded and good, or do I feel like I have shackles on and I'm constricted? Do I feel bigger, more loved and have freedom here, or do I feel small, wounded and insignificant? Does this person, place or thing make me feel like I am a gift, appreciated, loved and cared for? Or do I feel unappreciated, taken for granted, like I don't matter? Is this the best I can have? Or am I all that I can be? Does this bring out the best in me or the worst in me?

Be courageous enough to ask and answer these kinds of questions and you will find out whether you are in an environment that nurtures and supports you ... or an environment that tears you down.

Self-love comes when you learn to say **NO** to being a victim. What is being a victim? It's when you allow someone to talk to you in an abusive manner or in a way that doesn't feel good and is not empowering. Or when you allow someone to talk abusively to you or hurt you physically and you feel like you have no options, no control and no way out.

You do have control. You do have choices. There is a way out.

Did you ever see someone put their hand up and say, "talk to the hand, I'm not listening"? Here is a little script of self-love that you can say: "You cannot talk to me like this anymore. It is hurtful and not true." When you learn to stand up for yourself and realize you have a choice, you do not have to take abuse. You can say, "No. The way you are talking to me is not okay!" This is the beginning of self-love. (I actually wrote the word NO and the above script on my own hand, because I would freeze in the moment of abusive talk, and then I would look at my hand to be able to say it.)

If the person continues, just say, "I'm going now." Turn around and get out of there. Walk around the block or the office building (wherever you are). Do not get into your car and drive. If you need alone time, go outside or go someplace where you can shut the door. If the person cannot respect your need to separate yourself from their negative talk, then you must think about removing yourself from that relationship or environment, or see a therapist who can help you communicate.

Self-love is putting yourself in an environment that is loving and supportive. Self-love is saying "no" to disempowering put-downs or being around people who don't make you feel good. Self-love is saying "no" to a negative environment and "yes" to yourself by setting healthy boundaries.

As an experiment, take a day and notice how you talk to yourself. What a concept! Ask yourself, "What am I saying to myself?" All day long, whenever you notice you're talking to yourself silently, giving yourself silent messages, ask yourself: Is this loving, powerful, supportive self-talk? Am I a cheerleader for myself? Or am I a harsh critic? Am I the one that's being vicious to me, tearing myself down?

Are you saying, "I'm so stupid, I can't believe I did that again!" Or are you able to say to yourself: "What did I learn from this?" or "Wow. I'm noticing this is a pattern. I'm glad that I can see that. Now I can change it."

Watch your thoughts! Do you praise yourself or do you tear yourself down? Especially look for where you judge yourself and others! The breathing exercises I gave you earlier are important to help you create positive self-talk. Breathe in the light and acceptance, and let go of the negative self-talk and judgments. Breathe in love and light and let go of what no longer works. The more you can practice these little moments of breath work throughout the day, the more powerful your self-love and self talk will become.

LOVE REALLY IS STRONGER THAN FEAR.

You can stop your negative talk and replace it with positive self-talk, but this does not happen overnight. Be kind and gentle with yourself. Take baby steps. The best thing you can do is to become aware of your self-talk first. Choose to be gentle, loving and kind to yourself whenever you realize that you have some work to do in the area of self-talk. Let go of guilt, judgments, shame, or blame.

Put your hand on your heart and say out loud:

"I'm doing the best that I can with the amount of light that I have right now, and I am healing, growing and changing into my highest and best self."

9: SHAME BUBBLES

As a child, I spent a lot of time wondering about what it would feel like to kill my sister.

I never really liked her, especially since my mother made a habit of telling me that I was *supposed* to like her. Everybody seemed to like my sister, and that made me angry. People would stop us on the street to tell us how beautiful she was. They were right about that, which made it even worse.

My sister has a double row of eyelashes, which make her eyes absolutely gorgeous, simply striking. As a child, she drew a lot of attention. I just thought she looked like she had spiders on her eyes.

Whenever people talked about how gorgeous she was (and especially when Mamma did), I got so angry and was filled with so much hatred that I literally couldn't see straight. My mind got muddled. She became the ugliest person in the world to me.

I looked for chances to tease her and hurt her, and I took every chance I could get. I hurt so bad inside, and I wanted her to hurt just like me.

One day, I invited her to play a game with me. At this point, my sister was a very lonely girl, and so she was surprised that I was finally paying attention to her, and very happy to be invited to play with her big sister. She said yes instantly.

I filled up the bathroom sink with warm water and bubbles, and told my sister that this game was about who could eat the most bubbles. She would get to go first, which meant she would have a head start. As she leaned into the water, I grabbed her head, pushed it hard under the water, and held it there.

I thought maybe she would die right then and there, easily; but no, she squirmed and broke loose and gasped for air.

It breaks my heart now to think how innocent she was. She didn't even show any anger. She just shook her head to get rid of the water, coughed a few times, said she didn't want to play that game, and left.

I knew I had done something wrong. The guilt and shame grew bigger in me every day. I knew I was a very bad girl and that I deserved all the bad things that had happened to me. I knew in my heart that I deserved all the punishment I got for all the things Mamma found out about. (She didn't find out about that one, though.)

Then there was the afternoon I found my sister lying down, taking a nap. This feeling just came over me, like I was in a trance. I was just so mad that she had taken my Mamma away from me. I put the pillow over her head and held it down tightly. Within a few moments she started kicking and squirming. She got her head out from under the pillow just in time. To this day, my sister has a deep-seated fear about being smothered by a pillow. I'm still working on the guilt over that one.

I loved watching the rodeo, and my favorite part was the cowboy's skillful use of the bullwhip. I loved it so much I saved up the money to buy a beautiful cowhide bullwhip. I practiced and practiced for weeks, aiming for twigs on the tree or cans set on the rocks.

I talked Sue into being my assistant. I would get her to hold cigarette butts in her hand, and I really would whip them off without hurting her. One day she decided to quit before I was ready. She just walked away. I snapped that whip around her ankles and she fell down on the gravel, bloodying her knees. I dragged her back to me. Of course she tattled on me. I got in trouble and they took my bullwhip away. That was the end of that.

"I knew I was a very bad girl and that I deserved all the bad things that had happened to me."

I had no way to physically torture her anymore, so all that was left was emotional torture.

HEALING MODALITY: SELF-FORGIVENESS

Self-forgiveness is the number one, most powerful healing tool that I know. In order to prepare for the benefits of self-forgiveness, you need to practice the centering exercise in the first chapter. This is a prerequisite for deeper healing work like self-forgiveness. Forgiving yourself is a must. It means you are willing to let yourself off the hook.

Sometimes you have to forgive yourself more than once, especially with deep issues. Healing rarely happens overnight. In my case, I had to do many self-forgiveness exercises to reach the deep layers of my shame and guilt.

Sometimes self-forgiveness happens by pure grace, which is a miracle. I have experienced these miracles; in fact, I experience them every day and invite you to open yourself up to the possibility. Grace happens when our hearts are really ready to completely feel the pain that we have caused someone else. This is what is called repentance (changing direction with compassion).

When I felt remorse for causing someone pain (like my sister) it became a powerful moment for change. Feelings are paramount. This is the powerful ingredient for doing inner work. You cannot do it from your head alone. You need your head and your heart totally engaged, which means you are willing to feel the pain and be with it. Denial is not an option for healing to take place. Many of us have numbed out for years and it takes a while to get down to the place where change can happen, where healing happens, where miracles happen.

Exercise For Self-Forgiveness

This is a technique I learned while studying at the University of Santa Monica. It helped transform my life. Give yourself 20 minutes per issue. Start by lighting a candle. Ask to be divinely guided, directed, and protected. Use it to center yourself using intention and breath work. Connect to your own divinity. Invite your inner guide to assist you. Now, remember the incident that caused you pain in your heart; maybe you hurt someone close to you. Put your hand on your heart, remembering the incident from which you want to be healed, and use these specific words:

"I forgive myself for judging myself for ..."

For example, in my case I would say, "I forgive myself for judging myself as a terrible sister. I forgive myself for hurting my sister physically and making her cry. I forgive myself for judging myself for buying into the idea that I caused my sister irreparable emotional trauma. I forgive myself for judging myself for buying into the lie that I ruined my sister's life. I forgive myself for judging myself for being hateful, mean, nasty and horrible to my sister ..." All the time dropping into your heart and allow yourself to really feel deeply and sometimes cry. Now it's time to "re-frame" it. Re-framing means re-stating what was to what is or will be.

"The truth is I did the very best I could for the amount of light, love and understanding that I had at the time."

In my case, I would say, "The truth is I was a hurting little girl myself, and I didn't know any better. I did the very best I could to model the light and love that I had at the time and I am still growing. The truth is I've learned a lot about love and compassion from this experience. The truth is I really love my sister now. We have learned to forgive and love each other. The truth is I wouldn't be the person I am today if I hadn't gone through those experiences. I am grateful for the opportunity to learn how to love more deeply, to have more compassion and to give myself to others with ease and grace."

I would say this "re-frame" with my hand on my heart, using different variations of the same theme until I felt a deep stirring of my heart and soul.

For real healing to happen we need to find the emotional wounds that cause us pain ... then pour Unconditional Love into them ... and then re-frame the issue over and over ...[1]

We need to forgive ourselves—deeply.

---

1 This technique was developed by Ron and Mary Hulnick, PhD at University of Santa Monica in their Masters Program for Spiritual Psychology

10: DADDY'S LITTLE GIRL

I remember that my favorite song when I was growing up was "Daddy's Little Girl."

At Christmastime we would listen to the old Grundig radio, and whenever that song came up, I would light up like our Christmas tree and sing and dance to it.

I can still remember the day my daddy taught me how to dance, too. Following his instructions, I put my little feet on his big feet, my tiny hands in his big hands. The power of the connection with him swept me away. I was a princess that day. Even the memory of his gentle touch makes me weep as an adult. I believe that is because, outside of those dances, I have only a handful of memories of him (or Mamma) ever touching me at all as I was growing up.

Like me, you're probably wondering: Is that even possible? To write this chapter, I racked my brain: What other memories do I have of physical affection from my father? Here's what I came up with.

I can remember that loving moment, of waking up after I had fallen asleep in the car, that moment when Daddy's strong arms would pick me up and carry me into bed and tuck me in. I felt so loved then.

And I remember the very last time my Daddy picked me up and brought me to my bed, I was 15 years old. It was about three o'clock in the morning. I was parked in the driveway with my boyfriend. We were both passed out from drinking too much beer at my very first prom. That night, I had lost my virginity. We had parked in the graveyard and downed beer after beer; I'm sure I had several quarts of the stuff in my system.

When my Daddy picked me up I felt both love and sadness from him. Yes, I was still groggy and drunk, but I do remember his powerful arms lovingly holding me and tucking me into bed. That's the last loving touch of his that I can remember from my youth.

All the other memories I can summon up are memories of the two of us at a distance. I remember when I was seven years old, sitting in the bathroom doorway on the floor by my Daddy as he was shaving. He worked as a fireman at night and had an insurance company job during the day. He was usually exhausted, and I barely ever got to see him.

My Daddy

As he was shaving, I was saying, "Daddy, I miss you, I want to see you more."

He told me he would be retiring soon and we would go to Florida and I would see a lot more of him. But when we went to Florida Daddy ended up buying a bar (his dream come true), and running it was a lot of work.

He would be at the bar at night and sleep during the day, so I saw him even less than before. Just about every time I did see him, in the afternoon before he headed off to the bar, he would have a drink in his hand: scotch and soda.

After that, the ocean became my daddy. Nature is where I went for support and comfort.

~~~~~~~~~~

HEALING MODALITY: RELEASING PATTERNS AND SABOTEURS

This healing modality is about dealing with the patterns that were created in our childhood. Here is a recovery tool to help guide you to release old saboteurs and patterns that may have been causing you pain, may have emerged as blocks in your life.

Consider the seemingly simple experiences of being touched by a parent. When we have a healthy Mamma and we fall down, our Mamma picks us up and comforts us with love, giving us healthy touches. She kisses the boo-boo and makes it better, and we feel not only the physical touch but also the love from deep in her heart. We experience her love, the warmth of her hug, and we feel nurtured and loved. We start to heal.

When we have an unhealthy Mamma, though, we may get scared – not just scared for the moment, but also frozen in fearful patterns that continue into adulthood. Maybe when we fall down, Mamma does not comfort us with loving touches, but hits us and says something like, "What's the matter with you? I told you to be more careful!" This was the case with my Mamma.

I want you to imagine a healthy Mamma or a healthy Poppa who, when you fall down, comes to protect you, love you, and comfort you with healing touches. If you are comfortable with appeals to God or to your Higher Power, I suggest that you awaken that healing connection through prayer. You can also establish this healing connection with the bedtime meditation exercise you learned earlier, or through the breathing activities I've shared with you here.

(You can find more breathing and meditation activities on my website, which is www.dalebach.com)

Here's a variation that uses a prayerful appeal to the Higher Power. Find a place where you can get really quiet, a place where you can quiet your busy mind, so that you can get to a place of asking. Get clear on what it is you need help with. Maybe it's the pattern of being punished, or fear of taking risks, or paralyzed by an internal critic. You want to let this go and give it to God. Give it to your Higher Power. Surrender this pattern of pain; this saboteur that is blocking you, and ask, "Please help me heal that pain." Or pattern. Or emotion. You must ask from a very sincere, deep place in your heart, and then trust and let it go.

If you are willing to do an experiment try this one: go out into Nature. Put your back against a pine tree and put your bare feet on the ground. Ask the Creator of that pine tree, of the earth, of all that surrounds you, for help.

With your back against the pine tree and your feet in the earth, take a deep breath, and then imagine that you are becoming one with the tree and that your feet are one with the earth. Slowly breathe out the pain of your issue, surrender to the earth and the pine tree. Let Nature nurture you.

You can even do this in the bathtub at home. Imagine that the water is taking the pain away. Or, if you wish, you can go to the ocean, to a lake, or even to a waterfall to wash away the pain from the patterns that have been so hard to overcome. Invite the power of Nature to heal you.

Become like a little child and surrender to the safety of something bigger, larger, older than yourself, whether it is the pine tree, a mountain, a thundercloud, or any other expression of the natural force that sustains us all. Whether you believe in a Higher Power or not, remember that all life, including yours, traces back to the ocean. Remember where you came from. Remember the wave surrendering to the ocean. Let this memory, which is lodged deep in the cells of your own body guide you back to your wholeness.

11: BAR ROOM LOVE

My father adored my mother and was (so far as I can recall) completely obedient to her wishes. When, over a second cup of coffee on a Sunday morning, he would patiently answer my questions – about religion, or what made for a good life, or what happens after we die, or about anything else profound that I could think of – Mamma would listen patiently for a while, and then eventually tell him to stop gabbing because there was work to do. He would obey, smile, and stop talking. He then got up from the table and went to do the chores, or whatever. A little part of me always longed for another chance to see his eyes beam bright, to revel in him reveling in explaining the world to me.

He must have liked it, too, because whenever he would go out to run errands, I would be invited to go along with him. We would go to the post office, the grocery store, or wherever else was on the list my mother had set up for us. We would talk and I would have him all to myself, and Mamma wasn't there, ordering Daddy to stop talking.

During one of those drives, I remember him telling me that he never, ever, was alone; that he had a partner who never left him; that God was always on his left shoulder. He paused for a moment and let that one sink in; then he told me that whenever he had choices to make, he would ask his partner, the guy who was so close to him, what was the right thing to do. And then (he continued) he would get a feeling of knowing what was right

> "I remember him telling me that he never, ever, was alone; that he had a partner who never left him, that God was always on his left shoulder."

to do – and then he would follow through and do that.

That little talk in the car stayed with me, has stayed with me, all these years. It helped me to get the great, unreachable Catholic God out of the sky – maybe not inside my heart, but at least, at that moment, onto my left shoulder.

I fell in love with my father over and over again because of moments like that. In later years, I loved him just as much, more maybe, because I could see him as a man with both virtues and flaws: as a good provider, a hard worker, and a deeply loving husband and father on the one hand – and, on the other, as a high-functioning alcoholic who turned a blind eye to my mother's excesses and spent, perhaps, less time with us than he should. (My mother, too, was a high-functioning alcoholic, but that much may have been clear already.) My father was very human, as I am, and he had a deeply personal conception of spirituality, as I do.

On the way back from the post office or the store or wherever it was we had been, my Daddy would announce that it was time to stop at a Friendly Inn he knew of "to wet his whistle." That meant he would have a few beers at the bar, and I would be left alone in the car for an hour or two that seemed like an eternity. This pattern continued, weekend after weekend, until eventually I grew weary of waiting. One afternoon I got up out of the car to go into the bar and sit (illegally, I now realize) next to my Daddy.

Usually, he would order me a Shirley Temple and a Slim Jim. I really didn't like being in the bar with a bunch of smelly old men – who would at age nine? And I remember one ritual I particularly loathed. Some old drunken geezer would ask me to dance to a song he had put on the jukebox, and my Daddy would say, "Go dance with him." And I had to dance with an anonymous boozer. This is not what I wanted.

I see now how the pattern was created: a few amazing, precious moments of connection with my Daddy and then a feeling of being abandoned and left alone and ignored. Feeling so loved in one moment and so unloved in the next created a pattern that carried me through most of my adult relationships with men.

Yet even the ability to recognize that painful pattern in my own life gives me an unexpected affinity with him, years after his passing: We were both doing our best with what we had at the time. And we both knew we were accountable to God. I suspect he asked for forgiveness for the times he left me waiting in the car, for the times he made me dance with strangers, as I have asked for forgiveness for the mistakes I've made in my own life.

Whenever I looked into my father's eyes, and he looked back, all time stopped. He had the most spectacular crystal blue eyes. I could see and feel eternity when we looked at each other. It was as though he looked into my very soul, and when he did that, I felt profound, deep love and connection, truly soul-to-soul.

Those remarkable blue eyes put many people at ease. When Daddy walked through any door, the room would light up, and smiles would appear on people's faces. He used those eyes to empower people everywhere he went; he would notice something good about you and compliment you for it with deep emotion, all the while fixing you in his gaze with those blue eyes. He would put you at ease with those eyes, connect with you and make you laugh and share his great sense of humor with you. I can't remember ever seeing a frown on my Daddy's face. I remember him telling me that every day is a gift and that, throughout each day, he would constantly say "Thank you, thank you, thank you" to God for the many blessings and gifts that he had in his life.

I have learned to be grateful to God for everything in my life, even the dark times, and I believe I have my father to thank for that.

~~~~~~~~~~~~~

HEALING EXERCISE: Gratitude Book

When we are in gratitude there is a feeling of lightheartedness. Gratitude is one of the most powerful, necessary components for healing on all levels. I invite you to make a gratitude book for yourself.

Go out and buy a little journal you can use as your gratitude book. Perhaps you won't even have to buy one; you might find a blank notebook lying about the house. Or you could make one with paper and staples – draw something nice on the front like a happy face. Be creative and let your inner child decide what goes on the cover.

Think about what you are grateful for; think about all the things that you appreciate in your life. If you are not used to thinking of what you are grateful for or recognizing the good things that you have in your life, I want you to be grateful that you have 10 fingers and 10 toes. There are many people who do not. You have to start with the very basics. If you have two eyes, two ears, or even if you only have one ear, be grateful for everything you have on the physical level, the most basic level. Can you breathe? Is there air around you? Did you eat today? Do you have clean water to drink whenever you need it?

You get the idea. Every day, think of something for which you are grateful. Maybe you have a nice warm bed at night. Maybe you have friends whom you love and who love you, or family members you feel lucky to have in your live. Write it all down. List everything for which you are grateful.

This is how it goes: every night, list ten different things you are grateful for, and then read the ones you've already written. The more you do this, the more gratitude accumulates, until you start feeling happier.

If you get stumped, do a little bit of the centering exercise. Ask for help from your Inner Counselor. Imagine a time in your life when you felt really wonderful, perhaps – a time when you fell in love, or the day of the birth of your first child, or the day you were given a little puppy or a kitten; be willing to go way, way back when you are working on your gratitude book. Experiencing gratitude will bring up your vibration and make you feel happier overall. This is the benefit of the gratitude book.

12: "KILL ME NOW, GOD"

"God, please kill me now, while my soul is pure."

I was eight years old when I prayed this prayer. I was walking down the front steps of my church. I had just made confession.

I wanted to go to heaven, and to make absolutely sure that happened I wanted to die right then and there. I knew that by the time I walked home my soul would be black again from some sinful thought or deed, and if the moment of death came then, I would go to hell for sure. I knew I was not supposed to kill myself, but I had never actually heard anybody say anything against me praying earnestly for *God* to kill me. So I uttered this prayer with deep feeling. I really, truly wanted to die at that moment.

> *"Once we finally learn to forgive each other, we will have more peace, and so will the world."*

I had told the priest about all my sinful thoughts and actions, about all the awful things I had said, felt, and done to my mother and sister. I had said all the Hail Marys and Our Fathers I was supposed to. Now I felt such radiant light within me, through me, and all around me that I knew I had just been forgiven for all the horrible things in my heart. I was feeling the purest that I had ever felt as I walked down those stairs.

As I continued on my walk home I found a dead sparrow on the roadside. I picked it up and I made a prayer. I wanted to heal it. Realizing that it would not heal, I started to cry. This little bird had gone to heaven, and I had to stay behind to make more mistakes and keep feeling the gnawing pain of guilt, shame, and hopelessness. I felt a wave of great sadness unfold, beginning inside my solar plexus. I was so envious of that dead sparrow. Why did he get to go home and I had to stay, why was I left behind? I was the one who had just prayed for death. Did God make a mistake and take the sparrow to heaven and forget that I was the one who had asked to die?

I didn't know it then, but there is advice in the Bible about sparrows. What it says, more or less, is that God knows what He is doing. No sparrow falls to the ground without being part of His plan. That plan did not become clear to me until my fifties. But it was there all the time, guiding me.

One of my early mentors in my healing work was a woman named Dr. Jean Huston. After seeing me onstage, talking about my past and how I had come to terms with it, she said, "You are a peacemaker."

I accepted her compliment, but at the time, I really had no idea what she meant. It took a while for me to figure out what she meant. Now I know: God knew exactly what the plan was, why it made sense to take the sparrow and leave me on the earth for a while to learn and share what I had learned with others. God meant for me to be a peacemaker for mothers and their children, to help us to understand each other. Once we finally learn to forgive each other, we will have more peace, and so will the world.

~~~~~~~~~~~~

HEALING MODALITY: SEEK OUT MENTORS

I have learned to seek out mentors, and they have helped me make real breakthroughs. As I reflect upon my life I realize that I have had amazing mentors. Some are alive, some have been dead for centuries; some I know well, some I have only watched from afar. You don't have to sit down at a table with someone for that person to emerge as the perfect mentor for you at a certain stage of your life.

Listing all the mentors who have made a difference in my life is probably an impossible task, but a partial list would include, Jesus, Dr. Mikao Usui, Dr. Michael Beckwith, Louise Hay, Dr. Bruce Lipton, Neale Donald Walsch, Mark Victor Hansen, John Cleese, Oprah Winfrey, the Dalai Lama, Thich Nat Hanh, Divine Mother, Buddha, William Blake, Ralph Waldo Emerson, Benjamin Franklin, Carolyn Myss, Dr. Jean Houston, and many more.

For example, Dr. Jean Houston brought to my awareness that, indeed, the abuse and disconnection of my earlier life would become my opposite – a gift of peacemaking, especially between mothers and daughters (or mothers and sons). My hope for this book is to offer encouragement to others, to find compassion for themselves and others and to know that if they seek it they will indeed find it.

Think about the people who have really inspired you. Maybe it was Albert Einstein, or one of your teachers, or a coach, or a family member, whoever it was, take a moment to reflect upon the person, and then make a list of everyone who has already served as your mentor. When we go to a conference that inspires us, watch an uplifting movie or television program, or listen to the radio that is meant to inspire, teach or raise our consciousness ... when we read a book, or listen to an audio program; when we call up a friend who has experience we lack ... we are opening our minds to be influenced and inspired by a mentor.

We need to choose people who uplift and inspire us, give us courage and motivate us to think differently, who will move us into the greater parts of ourselves to give of our gifts, explore our greatness, or perhaps even be of service to others, maybe to help us become part of the solution for the healing of our earth, give people a hand up, share our gifts and knowledge, whomever, whatever can help us do this. Engage with them. Connect with these people and tap into their knowledge as often as possible. Allow them to mentor you through their programs, their teleconferences, their conferences, or if you are brave enough, by reaching out and asking for a meeting. If your mentor is inaccessible for some reason, though, you can also find the guidance through the written word, books, audio programs, and so on.

"Audio mentorship" has been a particularly powerful resource for me, and it can be for you, too. Whether your commute is for just a few minutes, or for an hour or more a day, start listening to audio programs in your car. I always use my car time to learn. It is as precious as the time I spent at the university. For over two decades I worked in the film industry and my commute would be at least one to three hours per day. Every day, I listened to audio programs that increased my understanding of emotional intelligence, and spiritual connection that helped me to heal myself from the victim mentality, and identify and understand life patterns so I could consciously change my life.

I have been diligent in my pursuit of emotional balance, mental clarity, spiritual connection, and physical health, and mentorship has been the key. I encourage you to find out what inspires you, who inspires you, and then find a way for them to be your mentor. Some people can grow and change alone, but I have found very few who have been successful at it. We all need each other. The reward for committing to the mentorship process is immense. You are worth it. Go forth and allow yourself to be truly inspired. It has been said that whomever you spend time with, you become like. I believe that to be literally true. So: whom are you choosing to hang out with?

13: A DAMNED YANKEE

In 1957, I was entering first grade. My family had just
moved to Venice, Florida. This was our fourth move. I was
excited about the first day of school, and I was certain that it
was going to be a great day. But I was wrong.

The trouble started early. My teacher, Mrs. Debnum,
asked each child in turn to stand up, say his or her name, and
say where he or she came from. When my turn came around, I
stood, said my name, and told the class that I had just moved
to Florida from New York City. Up until this moment, my
teacher had been pleasant and loving to the other students, all
of whom came from somewhere in the South. But when she
heard that I came from New York, her face reddened, her eyes
flashed with fire, and her mouth tensed.

She stared me down – remember, I was only seven – and
said, in front of the whole class, "You damn Yankee! It was you
Yankees that killed my grand pappy in the Civil War!"

The words sent shivers down my spine, and from that day
forward I was an outcast in grade school. Other children didn't
want to hang around me; if they did, they would be in the
banned "out" group with me. This pattern continued
throughout my high school years, as well – though not because

I was a Northerner. I always seemed to be in the "out" group, no matter what grade I was in. And my relationships with teachers were usually terrible.

In third grade, I remember my teacher, Mrs. Hill, getting the yardstick out and slapping my calves until they were red, welted, and swollen – because I was late to class and she wanted to teach me a lesson about tardiness. I couldn't remember her doing that to the other children just for being late.

It seemed like all the other girls were close and had friends. I was alone. I felt no one liked me or wanted to be my friend.

One promising day, I had a play date with Susan, a new friend, who had kindly invited me over to play a game of jacks at her house. We were sitting on the floor, playing. She was a real pro. In fact, she was winning by a large margin. I, on the other hand, I played very badly, and the better she did, the more I felt like judging and hating myself. I started getting very angry and went into a slight trance. I saw myself pick up two or three jacks and throw them into my mouth. One went all the way down and lodged in my throat. The trance suddenly lifted, and I realized what I had done ... because I couldn't breathe.

Susan screamed, "Help! Help! Dale swallowed a jack!" Her mother ran in and started pounding my back. I remember some man picked me up by my heels and was pounding my back to get the jack out while Susan's mother called mine on the phone. He must have dislodged the jack, because I could breathe again – barely – but it was still stuck in my throat.

My mother was usually a slow driver, but that day she drove so fast the police stopped her. When she explained what was happening, they turned on their siren and escorted us to the hospital.

It was all very scary, but some part of me was happy: She had me lie down with my head on her lap. I actually felt joy inside my heart because I finally got to be close to my mother. I had her lap back. I felt really special, because the policeman cared enough about me to put on his siren and get me to the hospital. I wouldn't die.

> *"It's amazing how desperate and creative I was to get my emotional needs met."*

We waited in the emergency room. I listened to my mother pleading that she needed the best doctor to take care of her little girl. She held me and nurtured me. I felt her love for me, for the first time since my sister was born. Finally the doctor arrived, and as they put the ether mask on my face, I remember feeling deep peace. I finally got reconnected to my Mamma.

After the surgery, the doctor showed me the jack that he had skillfully removed from my throat – without cutting into my flesh. I asked for the jack back so I could return it to Susan. The doctor refused, saying he had to frame it because he framed all his successes. (Looking back, I doubt she would have wanted the thing, anyway.)

It's amazing how desperate and creative I was to get my emotional needs met. Perhaps this is where the pattern of me creating accidents started. I needed the attention. I always found myself on the "outside," but I desperately craved being nurtured and loved.

I felt so disconnected at school that I decided I would just play deaf. It seemed that either the smart children got all the attention or the really stupid ones did. I didn't fall into either category, so I figured I would just drop out and stop listening.

After a few months, the school decided to give me some psychological tests. After all, it's not normal for a child to act like she cannot hear when she can. My responses to the testing gave the school officials some concern. They told my parents that I was emotionally disturbed and that I needed psychological care. They also tested my hearing. It was perfect; at least when my mother was not in the room. When she was in the room, though, I seemed to have very little hearing left.

In the years that followed, I concluded from the label "emotionally disturbed" that I was different, and as far as I was concerned it was not okay. Once again, I was an outcast. So I kept looking outside of myself to find the answers. It seemed the only thing to do, since I thought I was broken.

Something was really wrong. I would always ask other people's advice about what to do, about what I should think, and about how I should act, and what I should be. I thought everyone else knew much better than me. I had absolutely no self-confidence, no idea of who I was, and no sense of my own identity. I tried what "they" said ("they" being anyone who would let me ask a question) about what to do. I listened to "their" advice, and, usually, tried it "their" way. I had no ideas or opinions of my own, no concept of my own way of doing things, no experience thinking things through for myself. I continued with this pattern long into my adult life. I eventually discovered that I was actually betraying myself. I was giving all my power away to others – and getting myself into all kinds of trouble.

~~~~~~~~~~

HEALING MODALITY: WASH IT AWAY

Feeling like an outsider, like I didn't belong, left me
feeling contaminated. Maybe you've experienced that feeling,
too.

Believe it or not, drinking water is one of the simplest,
most effective ways to make a conscious choice to wash away a
feeling like that, a feeling that doesn't support you. While you
are pouring filtered, pure water into a glass ask your inner
divinity to make it holy water. Know that it is already done,
just by you asking. As you drink the water, imagine that you
are consciously washing away all the upset, all the anger, all
the sadness, all the depression, all the fear from your body.
Imagine the water is glowing, and as you drink, it goes into
your body and sends out a vibration of purifying and cleansing
light and energy to every cell of your body, into every organ
and every bone; right through your whole body into your auric
fields. You are choosing to drink for transformation.

I am not suggesting that you deny your feeling. Denial is
not healthy. What I am describing is just another way of
transforming emotions using intent and action.

Alternatively, you can take a shower and simply wash the
"bad" feelings out of your body. Imagine that the showerhead
is the most beautiful, healing waterfall in the universe. As you
put your body under that beautiful, cleansing, healing
waterfall, your body becomes a sacred sanctuary where you are
fully cleansed—in body, mind and spirit – whatever energy and

stuck thought forms, belief systems, or patterns that have been blocking you, hindering you and keeping you small. Imagine that all of that has been washed away in the shower. Do it with the intention of cleansing all parts of you and then after you feel like you're cleansed. While you are being cleansed and purified by your magic waterfall, call forth all the good things that you want to replace the fear.

This is the time to do some powerful affirmations. If you really want to get into "supercharged" mode, turn on the cold water and then say your affirmations. This will shock your body! It is great for your skin and it also amps up your emotional body, so that when you say an affirmation it really takes hold. Some great affirmations for the cold shower after the cleansing warm one are:

- Everything comes together for my highest and best good, now and always.

- All of my needs are met, now and always.

- I have all the money I need, and plenty to spare.

- Every day in every way my life is getting better, on all levels and all dimensions, right now.

- I love my life.

- I am worthy of love.

- I can do it!

- I am that I am!

- I love. I am loved. I am happy and free

- With every breath I take my body feels better and better

The benefits of taking a cold-water shower – the act of washing away – after cleansing in a warm shower are:

- It will supercharge your affirmations.

- It will awaken your best super-conscious and subconscious insights faster and more powerfully.

- It will lift you out of depression.

- It closes the pores on your skin and makes your skin healthier.

- It improves your circulation.

- It gives you more energy. It has many other health benefits

- It's a great way to change your emotional state from negative to positive – quickly.

When you use these powerful self-talk and affirmation tactics, you will reap huge rewards. Experiment with what I have outlined here. Try it at least once or twice. See how it feels. See for yourself whether it works for you. Most importantly, have fun!

14: OUTCASTS ON THE BEACH

There were a lot of things in my childhood that didn't make me happy. What did make me happy was going to the beach.

As I've mentioned, we lived in Venice, Florida from 1957 to 1961, when I was between the ages of 7 and 11. I never felt lonely at the beach, whether I had anyone to play with or not. Very often, I didn't; my folks weren't home during the day (they both worked), and most of the neighborhood parents wouldn't let their kids come over for play dates unless there was a grownup in the house.

I was more or less on my own, unless you counted my elder brother, which I usually didn't. Every day, while he watched my sister, my favorite thing to do was to go to the beach by myself and play. For more days than I could count, I would spend the available sunlight in and out of the gentle waves, all by myself, and as happy as the water was blue.

Eventually, I made friends with Donna.

Donna was my age. She had white-blond curly hair like mine, and dark skin from spending so much time in the sun. She always ran around without a top because (as she put it) the boys didn't have to wear tops, so why should she?

Donna was a rebel with a cause, her own individuality. Donna was the one girl who was allowed to play with me when my parents were at work. This was because her father was the lifeguard at the beach, so he could always keep an eye on her – and, of course, on me. I felt safe when he was watching us.

I received great kindness from Donna and her family. I remember having dinner at their home and feeling a sense of love and acceptance that I'd never felt before. Secretly, I wished they were my parents.

Like me, Donna and her family were outcasts. They were Christian Scientists. The whole town scorned them and called them murderers. Their six-year-old son had died of pneumonia; because of their strong religious beliefs, they had declined medical attention. This was why people said such terrible things about them, both behind their backs and to their faces.

I knew Donna's family had loved their son beyond words. When I finally learned why people in town were so cruel to them, I cried for them.

Donna and I became fast friends. She was a classic tomboy: strong, independent, and outspoken. She did not fit in with the other "girly" girls any more than I did. Together we spent hours finding shark's teeth on the water's edge of the Gulf of Mexico. We sold the sharks' teeth to tourists.

In Donna, I found something I think we all need – a friend who respects you for who you are, not who you're expected to be by other people; a friend who will stand up for you when the time comes. The time came for me just a few weeks after I met

Donna and fell in love with her family, and it happened on the beach we both loved.

Vicky was another of my beach friends. She wasn't as kind or nice as Donna, though. Vicky's mother was single and would always dress very sexy. She would drop Vicky off at the beach, leave her there to play, and pick her up at the end of the day. So we had that in common: our grownups were gone during the day.

One day, Vicky said something strange to me: "Look, I have a new quarter. Do you want a quarter?" I always wanted money.

I said, "Yes, sure, I want a quarter. What do I need to do?"

Vicky said, "Oh, just go out to the sandbar, and that man will give you a quarter if you sit on his lap."

I was a little uneasy about this. Something deep inside didn't feel right. Vicky assured me that it was easy money, though, so I decided to do it. (This was an example of me letting others guide me, rather than me listening to my own instincts about what was the right thing to do. This pattern, as I have mentioned, played out for decades.)

"Right out loud, she called him a dirty old man and ordered him not to touch me or any other of her friends — ever again."

I went out to the sandbar. The fat, wrinkled old man who was sitting out there told me that all I had to do was come and get the quarter. I just needed to sit on his lap for a minute. I did, and when I sat on his lap, I felt his finger go in between my legs to my private place, and it hurt.

I squirmed and said, "I have to go now." He said, "Okay, here's your quarter, come back and you'll get more." I felt so horrible and dirty. I knew this wasn't right.

I asked Vicky why she had told me that all I had to do was sit on his lap, when he did something that didn't feel right. She denied it all and called me crazy.

I told Donna what had happened. She got so upset that she ran straight over to the man and started to scream at him. Right out loud, she called him a dirty old man and ordered him not to touch me or any other of her friends – ever again. The old man got up, hung his head, folded the chair, and walked quickly off the beach. We didn't see him too much after that.

Donna was my hero. She stood up for me and protected me. No one had ever done that before.

~~~~~~~~~~~~~

HEALING MODALITY: LETTING GO OF TOXIC PEOPLE

Let's say you realize that the people you're hanging out with don't make you feel good. What do you do? Decide who you do want to hang out with.

Ask yourself: Do I feel like I have more energy when I am around these people, or do I feel more tired? Do I think better about myself when I'm around them or less about myself? Do they leave me feeling more healthy or unhealthy?

Every time we spend time around someone, that person influences us. Nowadays, I like to hang out with people who drink carrot juice and have fun having green tea. I made that choice. You can make your own choice. Supposedly, if you put a frog in a pot of water when the water's cold, and then raise it ever-so-slowly to a boil, the frog won't jump out, but will instead sit there and be boiled to death. On the other hand, people say that if you drop a frog into water that's already boiling, the frog will quickly jump out. The lesson: We can get used to ignoring stuff that can kill us, as long as we expose ourselves to it gradually. That's how denial works.

Look at your friends and see what they are doing with their lives and their time. Are they going in the direction you want to go? Do your friends validate and empower you or do they put you down and think it's funny? Are you sitting in a pot of water that is getting steadily warmer, and will eventually reach the boiling point ... without you even noticing?

Find new friends who empower you, support you, and want to see you succeed, friends who are healthy enough to want what is best for you. Learn to close the door to what you no longer want or are willing to accept in your life. When one door closes, another door really will open for you. I know this from personal experience!

Make a list of all your friends. Include your family, your co-workers, and your colleagues at work. Rate each of them with a number that shows how you feel when you're around that person: ten for feeling great, and zero for feeling horrible. Do this exercise with care and compassion, but do it truthfully.

Anyone who consistently ranks below five is a toxic friend or associate. You want to have friends who consistently rank at seven or above. Five to seven is marginal Four or lower means set boundaries and limit or eliminate your time with those people. Family members present special challenges, of course ... but everyone else who earns a four or lower, every time you do this exercise deserves an exit strategy.

You have to be willing to let go to grow. If you're not willing to let go of toxic people, then don't do this exercise! It will only put you in more conflict and pain. But at least be aware of who you are hanging out with. If you hang out in a rose garden, you will start to smell like a rose. If you hang out in the fertilizer, well, that's pretty nasty smelling.

Yes, we may need the fertilizer to grow, but once the lesson is learned and the gratitude is given, it's time to move on!

Remember: Whomever you hang out with you become like. Do you really want to be like the people you're hanging out with?

15: SHARKS IN THE WATER

I had my first crush when I was nine. He was a sixteen-year-old boy named Tommy. About three or four times a week, I would watch Tommy swim out into the ocean to where a group of small fishing boats had anchored. He was always welcome and the fishermen would invite him aboard.

I never saw anyone else join Tommy on his swims. I loved adventure, so I mustered up all my courage and approached him.

"Tommy, can I come along? I'm a great swimmer."

Tommy was tall, which meant he usually looked down at me. That's what he did this time. I got no answer. He just stared down at me. I repeated my request. "Tommy, no kidding, I could do it! It looks like a lot of fun."

"No," he said, "I don't need a tagalong with me." I was crushed. I pleaded with him. "Please! I won't be a bother to you. Please! I promise, cross my heart hope to die!"

In response, he gave me an icy cold piercing look that said, "Get lost, kid."

I didn't take no for an answer. When I really want something I go get it, or at least give it my best try. Some people call this stubbornness; I like the word *tenacity* better.

It was summertime and the sun was warm; the sand was pure white and the water sparkled like diamonds. At that time, I was at the beach every day by myself. I watched Tommy very closely and noticed that every time he would go out to swim to the boats he never looked back. That gave me a great idea. I made a plan.

That morning, I felt like a spy as I watched Tommy go into the water. I waited until he was out of hearing range, and then I slipped into the water and quietly swam behind him all the way until he climbed into a boat. I raised my arm and managed to yell, "Hi Tommy! It's me!" A look of disbelief and disgust crossed his face. It was not the big welcome smile I expected.

My heart sank as I realized I was an unwanted, uninvited guest. Two fishermen were drinking beer, minding their own business, and now they had me, a little kid, out of breath, wanting to be on their boat. I was an outcast again.

I said, "Please let me on your boat to catch my breath. I just need to rest before I swim back."

Their faces were impassive, but their body language showed me how unhappy they were. Even so, they said, "Okay, come on, little girl." I was exhausted; this was the first time I had ever tried to get to a fishing boat from the water. I could hardly get my body up over the side.

As I was climbing in, I cut my foot on the makeshift ladder. Blood started squirting all over the boat. I was mortified! They gave me an old fishing rag to try to stop the bleeding. It smelled like kerosene and fish guts. I pressed hard, but the bleeding did not stop.

"Oh, great," they said, "Now we have to take this little girl to shore." Their disgust was obvious. I stood up with my hands on my hips, and said, "Just let me catch my breath and then I will swim back by myself. I don't want to bother you."

They were relieved. "Are you sure, little girl?" I told them yes, I was. I felt so very guilty. All the trouble I had caused! Mamma was always saying I was just a pesky kid. Maybe Mamma was right. I felt terrible.

It was time to swim the long journey back to shore. I slowly got into the water, my bloody foot stinging from the salt water. It hurt a lot.

> *"Oh, God, I don't want to suffer. If that shark is going to get me, make it quick! But I promise, I will be a good girl if I live! Please, God, protect me!"*

I decided I would just do a sidestroke, and then maybe try a backstroke to get to shore. Right after I went into the water, they said to Tommy, "Go on, kid, follow your little girlfriend." He glared at me. I was so embarrassed.

He dove into the water, burst forward, and swam a little ahead of me. He turned around once and looked back at me when I was about eight feet behind him. He noticed a shark fin moving rapidly towards us and shouted "Shark!"

Tommy freaked out and started swimming as fast as he could. I turned around and saw what he saw. The shark was coming right at me.

I thought: "Oh, God, I don't want to suffer. If that shark is going to get me, make it quick! But I promise I will be a good girl if I live! Please, God, protect me!"

I never looked back. Neither did Tommy, who I could see was swimming like some supercharged Olympic champion. I just kept swimming and praying the whole way, talking to God. As I got closer to shore, I saw there was a crowd of people shouting and acting very excited. As I approached the shallow water, I could hear them shouting, "Look! Look at that dolphin going after that shark!"

Apparently, an angel had saved my life: a beautiful dolphin had protected me. I learned from the people on the beach that the dolphin had hit the nose of the shark with his nose! That ocean angel had distracted the shark from attacking me.

Surviving that swim back to shore was the great miracle of my youth. Tears roll down my face as I write this, even though I have told this story many times. To this day I jump up and down with joy like a five-year-old whenever I see a dolphin. I would not be here today if that dolphin had not saved me from the shark. I am forever grateful to the dolphins, the angels of the sea.

~~~~~~~~~~~~

HEALING MODALITY: Praying For Transformation and Protection

Prayer is the great protector. If you ever had issues with road rage when you're driving, I suggest that you pray the very first minute you get into the car. I'm very serious about this. Prayer has not only changed my life. Prayer has saved my life!

The minute I put the keys into my car I imagine a beautiful, radiant, golden bubble around my car. I ask that the loving God of the universe and all of the angels connected to love and peace surround my car and enter my mind and my heart. I place the intention of being a conscious, loving driver before God so I may be part of the solution instead of part of the problem.

Once you are on the road, have the intention of choosing your responses. If you see someone about to cut you off, you have a choice. You can think, "That so-and-so is cutting me off!" which will trigger a fight or flight response, which will in turn trigger dark echoes of all the pain, anger and violence you have experienced in your life. Or, you can look at the situation and think, "I choose to be loving, peaceful, generous, and kind. I will let that person in front of me because they're having a harder day than I am." You can choose whatever you want.

When you choose to stay within your bubble of Grace, you are making a difference and creating more Grace. By setting that intention and putting a protection bubble around your car, you are raising your vibration from fear to love. This must be a conscious choice. This is a "little" thing you can do that has a big impact. Choosing to create Grace makes your life happier, more peaceful and you will have more love in it.

I have found that I actually get more energy from being kind. It stimulates endorphins and serotonin in the brain, which gives a feeling of elation. Kindness feels a whole lot better than anger! And kindness, like anger, is contagious.

Just try it. Become a scientist. Do this as an experiment for one week. If you notice that you feel even a little bit better, then do it for another week. Soon, responding with kindness will be a conscious practice. You might just find a smile on your face more often than usual.

Here is my confession: I know all about road rage because years ago, I was the most violent road-rager I knew. I incited many drivers to become very upset—and even had highly dramatic moments of people threatening to kill me.

One time, when I was driving my daughters someplace (they were still very young), I heard them crying, "Mommy, Mommy, please stop driving so fast. You're scaring us!" I put my hand just under the little crystal guardian angel hanging from my rear view mirror. I didn't even touch it. My hand was about an inch away from the angel when it shattered, spraying tiny shards throughout the whole car – the angel just quit! My daughters' little mouths dropped open and so did mine. I said, "Okay, if our crystal guardian angel has quit, I better start being a better driver."

From that moment on I decided I had to pray every single time I got into the car. From that day forward, I was healed of road rage.

Prayers do work. Intentions are powerful. But they don't work unless you use them. (For more information about the power of prayer please see Chapter 31: The Power of Prayer).

16: RUNNING FOR MY LIFE

When I was eleven years old, tragedy struck. We moved from my favorite place on earth—our little house in Venice, Florida, half a block from the Gulf of Mexico—to what felt like another country: upstate New York.

I felt trapped. All the freedom I had found at the beach was stolen from me. All of a sudden, I had to wear heavy clothes to keep warm. There was a whole new school experience to deal with. Everything in my life was different. In New York, I found myself a stranger in a very strange, very cold land. There was one constant I knew I could always rely on, however: I could make my little sister's life miserable.

One day, a month or so after I had been plopped down in the middle of this new world, my sister, whom I had been taunting for years, did something I never expected. At the age of seven, she decided it was time to fight back.

We were alone in the house. I had, as usual, been teasing her mercilessly about something; I don't remember what it was anymore. All I remember was the shock of realizing that the impossible had happened: She had finally had enough! In response to something terrible I had said, she threw one of our big living room chairs on its side, and then she bolted into the kitchen. There, she grabbed the biggest butcher knife out of the drawer and ran towards me, her face red with rage, screaming, "I'm going to kill you!"

I ran for my life.

After I slammed the screen door and locked it, she slashed away at the screen with the knife for a few seconds, shredding it with startling ease. She reached through, unlocked the door, and quickly cornered me in the hallway by the front door.

> "Mom put my head through the wall!"

Both of us were panting from the chase. Her eyes were bulging. She lunged for me, and in an instant I was trapped. At my neck was the sharpest blade of the biggest knife we had in the house.

At that moment, Mom walked in, her arms laden with shopping bags. When she saw the big chair overturned, she dropped the bags and started screaming: "What the hell happened?"

My sister told her. Instead of her getting into trouble, *I* was the one who got in trouble. I didn't have a lot of time to defend myself, because before I knew it, my mom was running after me, screaming: "I hate you! I'm going to kill you!"

I ran for my life once again.

It was going to be close, I knew. I got as far as the porch, and almost made it all the way out of the house ... but then Mom reached out and grabbed me by my long, curly blonde hair. Time stopped. There was a moment of deep silence, as though I was in the eye of the darkest storm ever. My heart sank. I knew I was doomed. She yanked my hair from behind so hard that I heard a snap and felt a sharp pain in my neck. (A doctor eventually determined that it was whiplash.)

She kept saying, "I'm going to kill you," over and over again. And she did her very best to fulfill that promise, ramming my head clear through the quarter-inch-thick barrier of steel-grey shale shingles that lined our storm porch. As she slammed my head repeatedly through this stone shale wall, I yelled out my own bit of hormone-fueled insanity: "Go on, kill me; I dare you, kill me!"

This only fueled her rage, and accelerated the pace of her assault. It was as if all the anger and hatred and violence that my mother had ever experienced and repressed was being passed down to me—a legacy of hatred. The battering continued until she exhausted herself and threw me aside.

For the next few hours, I was (as a later generation would put it) "out of it." Time and space were out of sync. Yet I knew that something terrible had happened, that it had happened to me, and that my father needed to be told about it.

That night, when Dad came home, I went to him and said, "Dad, look at the hole in the wall. Mom put my head through the wall!" His face went pale.

He asked Mom in disbelief, "Is this true, Kitty? Did you do that?"

She ran upstairs. They must've had a talk about it, but nothing was ever said to me. In fact, her attack was never mentioned at all after that, except very briefly, as something that I had made up. She tried to deny that she had hurt me.

My head ached for over two weeks. I fell into a deep depression. I dreamed and prayed that my mother would die. I hated her more after that.

I decided that I had to get out of the house if I wanted to live to be an adult. It wasn't safe at home anymore.

I didn't die that day, but any shred of self-worth, confidence, and self-esteem within me did. I was not a girl anymore. I was a deeply fractured woman whose spiritual core had collapsed, whose soul was shredded like confetti.

This episode set up several unconscious patterns for most of my adult life: not feeling safe, especially in my home; looking for a man to save me; feeling unlovable; creating patterns of self-hatred and self-abuse; launching addictions to numb the pain; and, last but not least, experiencing countless "accidents" resulting in head injuries. I have had many concussions over the course of this life, injuries that made it very difficult to think straight and use logic on any level. I was wounded deeply in just a few moments; but the deepest injury, the one that took the better part of a lifetime to heal, was my addiction to anger.

~~~~~~~~~~~~

HEALING MODALITY: OVERCOMING ANGER

Anger is an extremely powerful emotion, one that deserves special attention from the person experiencing it.

Whenever you feel angry it is important to identify the emotion and notice where in your body you're feeling tension, constriction, or pain. You may feel it in your arms or legs, your stomach, your head, the center of your chest, or your throat. Becoming aware of where you are feeling bad is the first step to releasing anger in a healthy way.

When you feel angry, adrenaline pumps into your body. This triggers a "fight, flight or freeze" response. That is a physical phenomenon, not just a mental one, which is why it is so very important for you to be aware of your body in this moment. If you can identify the emotion as anger and identify where in your body it feels strongest, you may be able to learn to be neutral for a moment so you can assess the situation. If you can, you are way ahead of the game.

What is triggering your anger? Did someone stir anger in you because of something they said in a conversation? Are you feeling like a victim? Did someone just hurt you physically, mentally or emotionally? You need to practice posing and answering questions like these the *instant* you feel anger. This is a time to take a deep breath and connect to your inner being and ask, "What is the highest and best response here?"

You really do have a choice here. Your first reaction may be to go from your animal energy, which is your brain's response to lash out, to attack or to run. This is the smart thing to do if your life is in danger. Your animal survival mechanism kicks in and is in charge. More often, however, that is not the best response. Your anger is triggered, adrenaline shoots into your body, but there is no tiger after you.

Anger may be triggered from unresolved, old wounds and old pain that you have not yet addressed. As you learn, evolve and get closer to mastery of awareness of your emotions, you will realize that you have a choice whenever something anger-stirring happens. You can choose how you perceive this situation. Is it really dangerous? If it is dangerous, then running away or physically defending yourself makes sense ... but every situation is different.

By coming from a neutral place and then choosing a conscious response—by choosing to use your brain's right and left hemispheres, which means choosing to balance logic and emotion – you can make a better choice, a whole brain choice. Because I had trauma from physical violence and accidents, I developed PTSD (Post Traumatic Stress Disorder). My body was so used to the fight or flight reaction that when my anger was triggered, I would automatically go into a reactive mode. Logic and reason had nothing to do with my choices. I now know that my mother went through a very similar set of challenges.

For many years, when I experienced anger, I was incapable of taking a deep breath or counting to ten to calm myself down and get neutral. After many years of therapy and learning many techniques, I was able to respond more effectively: by removing myself from the situation, going into the other room, or taking a walk around the block to cool off. I found out much later that I had contributed to my "short fuse" and put unnecessary stress on my highly reactive nervous system by eating sugar to excess, and by making other nutritional mistakes. Since then, I've learned a lot about brain chemistry and about how to eat properly to calm my brain and restore my nervous system. Knowledge about what is and isn't healthy nutrition turns out to be very important if you want to have a balanced brain and a balanced life.

If we have not reached a place of mastery yet, anger can be an intense storm that leaves wreckage in its path. The left hemisphere of the brain is usually turned off and the right part of the brain, our emotional side, goes into reaction mode. This is not an evolved conscious response. When we react like this, instead of consciously responding to the situations we face, we may pay heavy consequences. We may say hurtful things to those we love, things that cannot be taken back. We may cause distance and upset in our relationships. We hurt ourselves in some way, or hurt someone else.

When we have emotional self-mastery, we are more "whole brained." The right and left hemispheres can work together, and we can ask ourselves better questions. For instance: "Is this is a positive person for me to be with right now?" "Is this a positive environment for me to be in right now?"

Once we have asked ourselves the right question, we can take appropriate action. We can either remove ourselves from the situation without drama, or take a moment to breathe, calm down and then have a conversation to find out what is really going on.

Lots of people tell me, "I've tried all that, but I still can't manage to control my anger." Once we dig a little deeper, though, we usually find out that the person has not really practiced the steps necessary for whole-brain responses to stressful situations. That's the way it is with anger. When it takes over our body, we convince ourselves that we've already exhausted every opportunity for managing it. Usually, we haven't.

If you feel you cannot gain mastery over your emotions, simply tell the other person that you need to leave the room to calm down, that you will be doing an exercise in the other room, and that you will be coming back more calm so you can have a better conversation. You may want to tell the person not to be alarmed if there are strange sounds. You're not hurting yourself or anything else but you are just releasing your anger in the safest way possible.

Go into a room where you can close the door and have some privacy. Then do the following exercise to release the anger that is already in your body.

EXERCISE: Conscious Temper Tantrum

Remember when you were two years old and you would get on the floor and have a tantrum? I am giving you permission to have a managed adult tantrum.

Lie down on a couch, on a bed, or even on the floor and close your eyes. Make a fist with each hand.

Bang on the bed, couch, or floor with your fists. (Don't hurt yourself.) Shake your head and your whole body as if you were saying, "No, no, no, no, no!" Try to make your whole body say, "No!" Or, if you need to, you can yell "No" out loud. If you need to do that, I would suggest that you put a washcloth or towel in your mouth, so when you yell you won't scare your family.

The point is to get the anger out of your body. You might hold your arm out straight to hit something soft (like your bed or a pillow or a rolled-up coat) so you won't hurt yourself. By using your fist and long arm strokes, you are getting the fight response out of your body. You can accomplish the same goal by taking a pillow and beat the bed with your pillow. While you're doing any of this, you can say something like, "I'm feeling really angry and I'm getting it out of my body now!"

A psychologist gave this exercise to me. It's amazingly effective. I used it quite often as I was recovering from my own Mamma Trauma. I would do it with my girls when they were younger. We would all be on the carpeted floor yelling "No, no, no!" together and shaking our heads as a two-year-old would. Most of the time we ended up laughing. We would often feel a bit exhausted, but emotionally much happier.

Don't just read about this and think that it sounds interesting, or sounds like something someone else should try. The truth is we all have anger issues. The important thing is to *do* the exercise ... not just read about it ... and get the poison of anger out of your body.

17: PRAYING FOR DEATH

When I was in my early twenties, I reached a point where I was literally praying for death. Every night, I'd go to sleep and say, "Dear God, please show me. Why am I here? What is my purpose?" I was living alone. I had just moved out from my live-in boyfriend's place and I was very unhappy. Night after night, I prayed for death.

I was completely fixated on death. I had death poetry all around me, and I was doing poetry readings around town in Hollywood. I'd get up and read these dramatic poems about death. People would come up and give me all kinds of praise about how interesting my story was and how painful, vivid, and emotional my writing was. I was getting praised for all the wrong things. I was focusing on the wrong things, and I was asking God for the wrong things.

There's a line in a Talking Heads song: "Watch out: You might get what you're after."

I had a dream one night in which I showed a teacher the book of my life. It was beautiful. The book was printed in beautiful colors. I was showing this authority figure how wonderful my life was. It was a nice dream, but when I woke up, I didn't feel like my life was all that wonderful.

The next night I went to bed and I said, "Dear God, just let me have another nice dream like that one, and make it clearer for me. Or kill me in my sleep. I don't want to live, unless you show me a real clear purpose for being here. It's too painful to live. So either show me a reason for hanging on, or just take me." It was a strange prayer. And it was answered in a strange way.

On Mother's Day, at 4 'o clock in the morning (I kid you not—it was Mother's Day!), a man came through my window, woke me up, and with a knife to my throat, said, "Do as I say or I'll kill you." I did what he said.

He was huge with massive hands; his eyes were red like a demon's. He quickly put a pillow over my head and hissed instructions. He violated my humanity. In that smothering darkness, I saw everything that had ever happened to me, I saw what was happening to me now, and I also saw my future spread out in front of me. Along that future, I saw two different paths from which to choose.

It was as if God was showing me that I had a choice about how to live the rest of my life. The path to the left showed me doing drugs, bingeing on alcohol, praying for my own destruction, and devoting my life to "numbing out." The path to the right showed me teaching people of all ages about love, forgiveness, and healing. I saw quite clearly that I had to take the path to my right. I saw that my purpose was to teach and show people how to harness their healing power and find peace.

All this happened while I was being raped. Yet as horrifying as that sounds, the reality is that that was the moment I decided what to do with the rest of my life. I was no longer praying to die. I wanted to live. I did what the rapist asked, for he was actually an answer to prayer. Dark and light were one.

He kept saying, "Stop shaking. Be still." But I couldn't. My body was shaking uncontrollably. He had his hand on my mouth so I wouldn't scream.

For a moment, while he was raping me, he took the pillow away. Strangely enough I was compelled to recite one of my poems to him. I said, "How High Must One Fly Before He Gets Suffocated in The Sky, and How Deep Must One Dive Before He Gets Buried Alive?"

I also told him I loved him. I know that sounds strange and it feels strange to me as I recall it, but it happened. (I have

> *"At that moment, he stopped raping me. He got up and got ready to leave. As he was heading for the door, I said, 'Do you need help?'"*

spent decades trying to discover why I said it and what it meant.) I wasn't condoning what he was doing. I was terrified and knew what he was doing was horribly wrong; but in that moment, part of me touched another dimension, a dimension where we were all brothers and sisters; that we all have a soul contract and we have to fulfill it. I was the victim. He was the bad guy. In this moment we were both dealing with a trauma from both of our realities. I had deep compassion for him—

there is no other word for it than compassion—as I realized that he, too, was deeply misguided, in unspeakable pain, profoundly out of balance, and wishing for death. Don't ask me how I knew all that, but I did. So I told him I loved him.

At that moment, he stopped raping me. He got up and got ready to leave. As he was heading for the door, I said, "Do you need help?"

That stopped him.

He shook his head and headed for the door again. Before he left, I said, "Don't do this to any other women. They're not as strong as me. They will not survive." He paused for just one more moment, and then left the apartment. I never saw him again.

For the next three weeks, I was pretty much catatonic. I had frequent hallucinations about the rape. It was as though I had been swept beneath a vast ocean and no longer knew which way was up. It took me over a year to get my bearings and start working my way back to the surface of my identity, to the journey I was meant to travel in my life.

According to Judith Lewis Herman, *Trauma and Recovery* (1992), "The ordinary response to atrocities is to banish them from consciousness ... Certain violations of the social compact are too terrible to utter aloud: this is the meaning of the word "unspeakable" ... Atrocities, however, refuse to be buried ... Remembering and telling the truth about terrible events are prerequisites for the restoration of the social order and for the healing of individual victims. When the truth is finally recognized, survivors can begin their recovery. But far too often secrecy prevails, and the story of the traumatic event surfaces not as a verbal narrative but as a symptom ..."

HEALING MODALITY: FINDING YOUR TREASURE

Give yourself between 20 minutes to an hour for this very powerful exercise.

Light a candle to create a sacred space. Take a few deep, cleansing breaths. Connect to your own divinity. Ask your inner guide to assist you for the deepest and most profound healing. Ask yourself, "Am I ready, willing and able to look for the hidden patterns that have been created in my life, the patterns that once served a purpose of protection?" Breathe deeply until you are ready to say, "I am ready. I commit to finding them. I am allowing them to be revealed and am bringing them into the light."

Now say this prayer:

Finding Your Treasure Prayer

Great Oneness, Divine Intelligence, I know that I am one with the power of Love, which is stronger than any other power in the universe. I surrender all fear, doubt, and trepidation to the power of Love and Light. I ask from the deepest part of my being for divine guidance, clarity and courage to look and find the patterns that have become destructive in my life. I am ready, willing and able to take the action of self-inquiry. I am choosing to go into my past to find the saboteurs and patterns that have kept me small, constricted, in pain, and in emotional bondage. I ask for the help of my Higher Self and Inner Counselor to help me with this.

Now, close your eyes. Review your life. Ask yourself about the patterns you have set up in your life. Take a deep breath, hold your breath for at least 15 seconds, and keep asking yourself to look closely at this question.

The reason you want to use this particular breathing method is that when you hold your breath in this way, it gets the complete attention of your subconscious mind. Your subconscious mind has the job of keeping you alive, which includes making your lungs work, your heart beat, and your blood circulate, and so on. When you stop the normal pattern of breathing you can make a direct command – which is what you are doing with these questions. The logical side of your brain, the left hemisphere, shuts down a bit, and the right hemisphere of your brain is activated. When you breathe like this, you have direct access to your subconscious where the answers about these patterns and their solutions are buried.

Many people report after doing this technique that they can't spell. That's good. That means it's working. That means the logical half of your brain is on hiatus for a little bit. That's what you want. Don't worry. It will come back!

You need to allow yourself time to let go and trust to be able to have this exercise work properly. Come from a neutral place. You need to let go of any ideas of the end result or preconceptions about the answers that will come your way. Simply go to a place of curiosity, a place of truly being neutral.

Again, close your eyes. Review your life. Ask, "What patterns have I set up in my life?" Take a deep breath; hold that breath for least 15 seconds. Keep asking yourself variations on this question:

What patterns have I set up in my life that I need to change to be happier and healthier?

Make sure you have a piece of paper and pen handy. After you've held your breath for a good 15 seconds, and as you release your breath, write down the first things that come to your mind. And if you find that you have forgotten how to spell, don't worry about it, just write down whatever you have as neatly as you possibly can so you can read it back later.

Repeat that process a few times.

Now, using the same breathing technique, hold your breath and ask the second question, remembering to hold your breath for at least 15 seconds. Ask this question over and over:

What do I need to let go of?

Again, the minute you let your breath out, start writing down the answer. Continue posing this question a few more times.

Here comes the third question. Remember to keep using the same technique of taking a deep breath, holding it for at least 15 seconds, while repeating the question, and then writing down the answers you receive.

What is the best healing technique that's in this book that can help me do this now?

Now that you have asked the questions and gotten the answers, it is time to say thank you, which is a very important part of this and all healing processes. Go into the deep place in your heart and say thank you to your Higher Self, your Inner Counselor, and all the helpers that have helped you. Truly appreciate them and give thanks with sincere, deep gratitude.

Once you have identified one or more patterns, you will know where your most important work lies.

I have to emphasize how important it is that you do all of this work from a neutral place, acting as though you were a scientist. If you are skeptical, that's great. Do what you have read here as an experiment and see for yourself whether it works for you. Some of the exercises I've shared will work for you and some may not. My suggestion is simple: Do what works and let go of what doesn't.

Do your best ... and let God do the rest.

18: POP! YOU'RE DEAD

I was paddling off the shore of another, equally fateful beach; paddling toward the far horizon with all the strength I had – pushing for a finish line I knew I could never reach. A huge wave rose up in front of me, and then there was a sound, the last sound I expected to hear out there on the open water. It sounded like a loud POP.

That's what I heard: POP! The odd sound lasted just long enough for me to realize that it was my own neck that had made the noise. I felt the vast, cold wave slam my body toward the ocean floor. Suddenly, everything was silent. An intense, sharp, pain jolted my entire body, radiating out from my neck and spine. Then, in an instant, the pain was gone, and I was gone, too.

Floating, somehow, above the ocean, I looked down at my lifeless body. It had floated back to the surface. The waves tossed it around like a rag doll. I clearly remember the flash of recognition: "My God. That's my body down there. It looks dead."

Next to my lifeless body, I could see the blue and white boogie board I had been using. It was bobbing like a piece of driftwood. The waves pushed it back and forth. It was now a quiet marker: "Look what happened here."

Being able to see such a scene, vividly and from a great height, did not seem odd to me at all. In fact, I felt a great peace, a peace that I had never felt before in my entire life. I no longer felt any pain at all. I felt utterly free.

The next part may seem too much like a cliché; but it really happened.

I felt myself, found myself, and sensed myself approaching this intense white light. I had no fear of death. Death felt like freedom to me. Everything was beautiful ... until the moment I heard the Voice.

The Voice was recognizably male – a detail that still puzzles me – and it was deeply authoritative; the most authoritative voice I had ever heard. It was a familiar voice.

"You're going out with a broken back and neck this time."

This soul-cry was far more intense than anything else I had ever experienced. The moment I heard those words from the Voice, I became aware that I had neglected to do something

> *"You're going out with a broken back and neck this time."*

very important in this lifetime. Now, everything in me was pleading for my life, because I knew I had not accomplished all I was supposed to do, and I could not leave before I had completed this important mission.

My soul screamed to the Voice: "I have to have babies! I can't die now! I have to have babies!"

The only fear I felt now was the fear of leaving my life without having had children. The only outcome I was focused on now was winning my life back, so I could become a mother. I could not leave without fulfilling my destiny. Leaving this life without children was simply impossible for me to accept.

In the very next moment, I was thrown back into my dense, physical body, now wracked with pain. I gasped and sputtered and breathed again, managing somehow to get my nose and mouth above the water line.

The Voice commanded sternly: "Then do it!"

I was in great pain, but all I could think of was that I had gotten a second chance. "Thank you, thank you, thank you," I said, over and over. A strange mixture of feelings resonated within me: gratitude, exaltation and humility. Complicating it all was the searing pain in my body. My fiancé—the man who was to become the father of my children—swam over and asked if I was all right.

~~~~~~~~~~~~~

HEALING MODALITY: OPENING YOUR HEART CHAKRA

The amount of happiness that you have depends on the amount of freedom you have in your heart.

— Thich Nhat Hanh

Our heart chakra is an energy center. You cannot see it with your eyes, but you can feel it and sense it. When we have had a lot of trauma and pain in our lives, this center closes down.

My heart chakra was closed for many years and truly did not open on a deep, powerful level until I experienced the amazing gift of having babies. Most people do not have their heart chakra shut down to degree that mine did. Because of all the violence in my life, my mind was closed and my heart was closed.

When your heart chakra is open, you are able to feel Unconditional Love, Joy, and Peace. You can have the freedom for which your soul yearns. You don't need to have babies to be able to open your heart chakra!

Here are some exercises to try.

Set aside between ten and thirty minutes of quiet time. Create a sacred space by lighting a candle. Center yourself internally. Invite your guides or angels to assist you. Sit with your feet on floor, back straight, legs uncrossed, and connect with your breath to your own Divinity in the center of your chest.

REMINDER: To center yourself, take in a deep breath as if you were breathing into the center of your heart. Hold it for three seconds with the intention of connecting to Divinity. As you do this, let go of things. Very slowly, let go completely. Then slowly breathe out through your mouth, emptying out. On your next breath, breathe in light, love and peace. Hold that breath for a moment and feel it in every cell of your body. When you release it, imagine that you are breathing out with intention to the center of the earth. Breathe in light. Breathe out anything that would block the light. Center yourself inside the center of your heart space with the intention of connecting to your Higher Power, to God, to Divine Intelligence, or whatever you use for Divinity. Connect to that now.

After you have connected to your own Divinity with your breathing exercises, imagine that, in the center of your chest, there is an iridescent golden pink energy bubble, with tinges of green. It is round, soft, and warm; it permeates the center of your chest.

Now imagine this energy bubble being filled with magic stardust that has the power to soften and open your heart chakra. Ask your heart chakra to expand and open. This may be a new experience so be open to feeling different kinds of sensations. You are now opening up into the fourth dimension, which is a non-material place of existence. This is a dimension that you cannot see, but you can certainly feel it.

ROUND 1: While breathing in and out as if through the center of your chest, say:

"I am merging my heart chakra and feeling the resonance of my own Divinity and Unconditional Love."

Do this for three relaxed, long, full breaths.

ROUND 2: While breathing in and out as if through the center of your chest, say:

"I am feeling and entering into full resonance with Unconditional Love."

Breathe this in and out through your heart center for three more long breaths.

ROUND 3: As you breathe in and out three times, connect your breath with your own Divinity with strong intention to resonate. Say and feel these words deeply:

"I Am Unconditional Love."

With this exercise you are knocking on the door of Love. Let Love answer.

If your heart chakra has been heavily blocked, you may not feel much at first. Continue to do the exercise anyway. Think of it as a spiritual sit-up. Trust and know that your heart will and must open. Love is your natural state of being.

As you continue to experiment with this and other exercises in this book you will continue to evolve, grow, heal and have a much happier life. Remember, love is more powerful than fear. It is your choice to consciously practice love. As you do so, you are consciously taking back your power. Love is the highest vibration there is. When you connect to Love on a daily basis, you are moving toward the place of actualizing and receiving the very best that love and life have to offer. Be sure to end the exercise with deep appreciation and gratitude.

19: A MOTHER'S LOVE

Early in my thirties, I found myself alone with my mother and the ocean at Johnson Shoals, Florida. We shared a lifelong love of the ocean: It calmed our fiery spirits. On the morning I'm thinking of, we were on the shore together, collecting seashells.

The rhythm of the waves lapping on the shore slowed down our racing hearts and healed our ragged souls. The sun's warmth was thawing our icy relationship. I remember thinking, as we collected our shells, that I finally felt safe with my mother. I began to see who she really was. She was not a terrible monster. I saw light emanating from her eyes and around her skin. She was a beautiful soul.

She saw beauty in even the most common seashell. We would find rainbows in the oyster shells, marveling over their beauty and appreciating the gifts the ocean was giving to us. Finally, Mamma was teaching me how to find beauty, how to see it, embrace it, and how to be present with beauty. This was a turning point. I saw her beautiful heart and our healing began at that moment.

As we continued to bend down and find the shells, listening to the waves on the shore, connecting with Divine

Beauty, my mother looked at me with great pride. I felt her love and understood our connection. Mother loved the ocean just as I did. There was something that we shared, after all.

Dale and Mamma at Johnson Shoals, Florida

During the hottest part of the day, we sat down and talked about how sore our backs were. I was in my thirties, Mamma in her sixties, but we could share similar stories about our backs. Something else we could share! We watched the sunset together, enjoying each other's company for the first time in our lives. She was so happy, as was I, that we had finally found a common moment together. It was sweet and precious. The hate I had in my heart finally started to melt away, and salty tears of forgiveness cleared my eyes.

I still have the shells we collected that day, and I treasure them.

Allowing myself to feel compassion and love for my mother was the beginning of the process of opening myself to the idea of motherhood. Through most of my life, I had never liked children and felt uncomfortable when they were around. I used to mistreat my dolls, lose their clothes or chop off their hair and drag them through the dirt. But I knew now that I couldn't leave this life until I learned unconditional love. It had only been recently that my soul was awakened to the fact that I had to have babies to learn unconditional love. That was a foreign concept at the time!

Having a baby changed everything. Miracles happened. The first miracle was that I felt blessed and grateful for the opportunity to be a mother. This was the most beautiful, direct experience of unconditional love in my life. I chose natural childbirth because I wanted to experience every pain and every contraction. When my baby's head started to emerge from the birth canal, I had a mystical experience. I felt as though I was one with Mother Earth. I felt the earth quake, pull apart and form a deep rift to the center of the earth and beyond. The miracle of life came from the center of the universe through my body. My heart became wider than the ocean. From the center of the deepest part of my being, emerged a pure radiant light that was my baby.

When I first saw Baby Ingrid, I felt unconditional love in every cell of my being, and it began to pour through my body into space, and expand out into the universe. I never thought it was possible to feel this profound, magnificent love. I had a connection with my beautiful daughter, and in that moment, I felt my heart connect to my mother.

The day I brought Ingrid home, exhausted from a three-day labor, my loving husband propped up a bunch of pillows against the wall for me. I tried to breast-feed her. My milk came out so fast that it squirted four feet across the room. I tried again and it shot out so fast, it gagged her. She started to scream. I felt sheer panic. I threw the baby over my shoulder to burp her and knocked her head against the wall. Oh my God! She started screaming louder. It was a strange karmic joke that bumped head. (Fortunately, I didn't do any permanent damage. Ingrid grew up to be a UC Berkeley grad on full scholarship.)

When my Mom visited and held my child in her arms, I saw this loving light pour out from her into my precious daughter. I knew that at one time she had held me like that, too. My heart opened a little more, and I felt real forgiveness for my mother.

As I grew accustomed to breast-feeding my daughter, I had another mystical experience. I felt like a youthful goddess who was also half-cow with this elixir of eternal life and love flowing through my milk. My heart chakra opened wider than I ever thought possible. In that moment, I connected to the Divine Mother. I was filled with gratitude that I got to experience this divine, magnificent sacrament of being a mother. I now know that a mother's love is truly unconditional love.

The sacred act of birth allowed me to realize the miracle of life. It was the first time I ever felt pure joy.

~~~~~~~~~~~~~

HEALING MODALITY: RAINBOW HUNTING

This exercise will help you to awaken your spiritual insight and connect with beauty, an aspect of the Divine.

Many of us go through life rushing from one place to another, never taking time to stop and smell the flowers – let alone look for rainbows. With practice, you can learn to awaken your senses and heighten your ability to find beauty, and you can awaken your spiritual insight, too, just by changing what you pay attention to.

People say that what you spend your time focusing on, you become. So what would happen if you spent more time focusing on beauty?

I invite you to look for rainbows. Like a five-year-old child, be curious and see if you can find three rainbows per day. You think that's impossible? Have you ever looked at clean hair in the sunlight? I challenge you to find rainbows in the hair on your arms, your eyelashes, in the hair on your head or someone close to you. Now, what does that look like?

If you are a woman who wears mascara, take the mascara off, and then go outside where the sun is shining. Close your eyes and look toward the sun. Barely open your eyes. Really look to see whether there's a rainbow on your eyelashes. I guarantee you it's there. I know because I've done this hundreds and hundreds of times.

The very first meditation I ever did when I was a child was on the beach in Venice, Florida. I would rainbow-gaze at my eyelashes for at least 20 minutes at a time. I've kept it up all these years, and it is now a source of great peace and joy for me.

The idea is this: rainbows are beautiful. They say that a rainbow represents God's promise for a better day. Maybe that's why it's hard to be depressed while you're really looking at a rainbow.

Open your heart to your own rainbow and let it come into your heart. When you find your very first rainbow, celebrate it like a little kid who gets all excited. Jump up and down. Don't be afraid to be silly. It is necessary to be silly here.

The easiest place to find a rainbow is a crystal. Crystals have lots of rainbows, but sometimes you have to put your eyeball really close to them and keep moving it in the sun if you want to see them. At a certain angle, you will find a rainbow in the crystal. If you look closely at the petals of a flower, you can usually find one there, too.

Finding a rainbow that invites you to become one with its beautiful light can elevate your whole mood. It makes you feel really happy. My challenge to you is to feel that childlike happiness, to find a rainbow and have fun. Do this to awaken the joy within you.

When my mother and I were on that little island in Florida, we were hunting for rainbows in the seashells. It helped us heal. We were bonding in Beauty. Beauty is a very powerful healing tool. Take advantage of it.

If your mother is around and you think she might be up for having some fun with you, see if you can find the rainbows in each other's hair. And if she's not around, or she is not up to doing this with you, then close your eyes and imagine your mother. Picture yourself finding rainbows in her hair. See them in your heart and take three deep breaths connecting your heart with your Mamma's heart. Allow the blessing of the rainbow and Beauty to heal you both.

20: STOP! REWIND! TAKE TWO!

It was a hot, humid summer day in Florida. I was waiting in a blistering-hot parking lot for my mother, sister and niece. They were late.

With my seven-year-old daughter, Ingrid, I had traveled all the way from California to visit my mother, and we had devoted the day to one of mom's favorite activities – shopping. My mother had gone one way in the mall with my sister and my niece, and Ingrid and I had gone another way. The plan was to meet back at the parking lot in ninety minutes. I checked my watch for what felt like the hundredth time: 121 minutes had passed.

Something snapped in my brain.

The Mommy Monster took over – a horrible, uncontrollable feeling. There was no place to hide, no place to run. Angry, jealous, resentful thoughts flooded my mind. During my 30 minutes of waiting with a small child in the hot sun, my hormones pushed my shadow-self into full control of my thoughts, emotions, and words. Adrenaline pumped through my veins; any thread of logic or sanity was missing in action. I suppose I should mention that, at this point in my life, I was going through menopause.

Once my brain snapped at that one hundred twenty-first minute, I went right over the edge of rationality – with my daughter as a witness. I was wandering around the parking lot, threading my way through the rows of parked cars, literally looking for cracks I could step on to "break my mother's back". I wasn't just mad as in angry. I was mad as in crazy.

A part of me was watching this scary, illogical behavior from a distance, and that part of me was feeling helpless. The dark part of me was in charge, my poor daughter in tow.

I finally found my way back to the spot where we were to meet, and in a few minutes they arrived, laughing and joking as though nothing at all were wrong. Taking deep breaths, trying to find some kind of balance, I heard horrible words leap out of my throat. They were daggers, these words, and they were directed at my sister. The minute they left my mouth, I

> *"I couldn't hold the rage back any longer. It was like trying to hold back vomit."*

knew I had made a mistake. I wanted to find a way to step back from the darkness. But I couldn't.

The old wounds had festered, but fortunately both my sister and I were in therapy now, so I quickly apologized and asked to talk with her privately, away from the rest of the family. We were beginning to make some progress, beginning to own our own upsets ... when Mom barged in.

We politely asked her to disengage, pleaded with her to let us deal with the problem ourselves, and promised her that we were okay. But she insisted on intervening. She not only intruded on our conversation – a delicate one – but took my sister's side and started berating me.

My shadow-self rose up again in a fury: "Mom, butt out!"

She kept on talking, completely ignoring me. She continued to put me down. I couldn't hold the rage back any longer. It was like trying to hold back vomit.

I heard myself shriek, "You have been one fuck of a mother!"

It shocked me. I had never used swear words around her ever before. It shocked her, too. Her shriveled-up, 70-something little hand smacked my face as hard as she could.

For the first time in my life, I slapped her back. Whack! It felt so good to get her back for all those years, for all those times she had slapped my face.

She did a dramatic spin, dropped to one knee on the ground, grabbed for her nitroglycerin, and feigned a heart attack.

After all the years of her drama, I knew she was faking it.

She fished a pill out of her purse, put the pill in her mouth, struggled up, and then raised her hand to hit me again. I could feel all the progress she and I had made, all the years I had worked in therapy, and all the thousands of dollars I had spent, flying right out the window.

My sister was crying, jumping up and down, saying, "Please stop!" She moved our innocent little girls away from the unbelievable scene of Mamma/Aunt Dale hitting

Grandma; having a knockdown, drag-out, honest-to-goodness street fight.

I grabbed Mom's hand – hard. I looked straight into her eyes and said, "Bitch, you touch me again and you die." She grabbed again at her heart, and slumped to the ground, sobbing on the hot concrete parking lot floor, getting another nitroglycerin tablet, putting it under her tongue as fast as she could.

"Die, bitch, die," I screamed, towering over her. "You have been threatening to die, all these years, now, do it! Go on, I dare you, die right here, right now!"

When violence takes over, it is as if you are stuck in a tar pit. You can't get out. Then you are the tar baby; anyone who tries to help you will get pulled in and get stuck. The only way out is to catch yourself before you fall into the pit. That's why you need to create a daily routine that supports your new way of being – to make the new way of being a habit. The more you practice the better you get at consciously choosing to change your life – one thought, one breath, one intention, one word, and one action at a time.

~~~~~~~~~~~~

HEALING MODALITY: BUILD A STRONG SPIRITUAL CORE

This exercise is especially good for those of us with a broken or shattered core.

1. Start every day with a prayer, or intention. Using your breath, focus your intention to connect to your own Divinity with deep gratitude. Breathe with the intention to connect to your own divinity. You may ask for help to connect to your Higher Power, God, guardian angel, Christ, Buddha, Allah, your spirit guides, or angels connected to the Highest Source of Love, Light, and service to assist you in having a deep connection. Breath in this Divinity in the center of your heart – merge your heart with Divinity's heart. Become One – feel the Love, the connection, Freedom, and Peace – this is your birthright. If at first you can't feel it, imagine that you feel it. After you practice this and imagine this, it will become real.

2. Put your hands on your heart and say thank you for this life – think of three things you are grateful for; your eyesight, your fingers, teeth, your bed, having a partner – whatever it is, connect and feel the gratitude in your heart. Think of a time in your life when you were less fortunate. Get the contrast going, and do whatever you need to do to feel grateful. Eventually you will feel Joy bubbling up from deep within your heart.

3. Ask your Higher Power to help you remember to choose loving thoughts, words, and actions today, and to help you to quickly forgive yourself and others if fear is chosen instead.

4. Imagine all the things that you want to do on this new day with the people, places, and things. See, feel, hear; make this like a little movie in your head and see the end of the day with you feeling happy and successful. Feel gratitude in your heart. Amp up the emotion of happiness and with a grateful heart take in a deep breath, hold it for a few moments, and let it go with complete trust that you are creating a new way of being with your thoughts, breath, intention and a will that connects to Divine will.

5. Take two. In the film industry, they always do more than one take; so we, too, will reframe the movie of our life by creating a different ending. At the end of the day, imagine the day as it played out – where you did things that felt off. Then, take two! Do it again.

Let's look at the example of me losing it with my mother in the parking lot, and let's see how I can "take two." I imagine the day as it was until the point where I started to feel upset. Then, I imagine it the way I really wanted it to go from a loving place. I ask God and my guardian angel to help me. I take a few deep breaths and start some healthy inner dialogue: "I am safe," "I am okay," "I am not a lost child," "They are on their way," "All is well."

I am able to change the fight-or-flight response by intention, prayer, and choosing to think different thoughts. Using deep breaths, in and out, through my heart – to be present and look at my precious, beautiful little girl and maybe ask her if she wants a treat like ice cream while we wait. I see myself choosing to take positive loving action; then I see myself and my daughter having fun and laughing and then meeting my sister and mother, hugging them and all of us going out for a lovely time shopping and having fun. Then I celebrate the victory, choosing to let go of the victim role – by visualizing something more supportive. I rewrite the script of my life at the end of the day. I imagine it, I celebrate it, and I let my heart be filled with gratitude.

Why does this work? It works because the subconscious mind will program whatever we *regularly* plant in it. If we plant new seeds and water them on a daily basis we will have a new garden; we will also have plenty of time to pull out any weeds we happen to find.

21: LETTING GO

Mamma lived. She never hit me again, but I had ruined the family reunion.

The whole family was convinced there was something really wrong with me after that. All I knew for sure was that I felt terrible, and that there was something that I needed to talk through with someone. But as therapy seemed to have failed me, I decided to go to my spiritual counselor, Reverend Michael Beckwith.

I told him the story, leaving nothing out, and shared with him how profoundly guilty and ashamed I felt about what I had done. He became very still. After a long pause, he looked me straight in the eyes and said, "Let it go."

He said, "Even Christ got mad."

I hadn't thought about that.

He told me the story about Jesus cursing a fig tree after it had failed to give him the fig he wanted. This mystified the disciples, especially when the fig tree died right after that! The point I took away from that story was that anger may be part of being human, but it is not something to hold onto.

"Let it go," he repeated. "Just don't do it again. Forgive yourself. Let it go."

It was good advice. I healed. I forgave myself, and eventually, I forgave Mamma. (I apologized to her, too.) The best part happened about seven years later.

I was with my mother, doing two of the things she loves to do best: shopping at a gem show and bonding over eating. We sat down at the snack bar, feasting on her favorite food, Nathan's hot dogs. We reminisced and remembered the details of the parking lot incident. I apologized once again, and Mamma did, too. We talked about the whole crazy event. What had seemed tragic and impossibly painful at the time now seemed funny. Who would have thought that was possible?

We had such deep belly laughs that we had to hold our stomachs as tears rolled down our cheeks. We almost fell off our chairs. We healed, that day, as we found the power of humor and laughter together. Granted, it was very dark humor. But it worked. We forgave – we laughed – and we loved.

> *"We are not victims! We are just volunteers for a dramatic performance that we get to star in, write, direct, and produce."*

We all have tough moments. We all have to learn to let go, find the humor, and celebrate the victory of moving beyond victimhood. We are not victims! We are just volunteers for a dramatic performance that we get to star in, write, direct, and produce. We can change the plot and make a tragedy into a comedy if we choose.

I learned a lesson about compassion as I reflected on that parking lot experience. After going through the ordeal, I really understood what the "Mommy Monster" reality was all about. I experienced the "Mommy Monster" for myself. Deep forgiveness grew in my heart for every time my mother had "lost it" with me as a child. I really understood a dark thread in her life, not just in my head, but also in my heart, and in every cell of my body.

Once you experience something that deeply, that personally, that intimately, forgiveness becomes more than a word. It becomes completeness. It becomes part of your identity.

I believe we are spiritual beings having a human experience. When we embrace our shadow with loving kindness and compassion we are healed with the memory of our own wholeness. Suddenly we are not dust but stardust, a rainbow in a cracked mirror. All of a sudden, we embody qualities like deep understanding, humility, compassion, forgiveness, love, accountability, empowerment, and personal transformation.

My hope is that you do not have to go through what I went through to get that feeling. My hope is that, by reading about a situation like mine, you will get the same healing transformation, the same kind of understanding that I got about what makes people go violent – and how compassion can emerge and forgiveness can happen between two souls, even in the aftermath of violence.

HEALING MODALITY: SHAKE IT OFF

When we hold anger, frustration or hurt inside, it can make us very sick. When we have past trauma, violence or heartache, remembering it or even watching something like it on television or in a movie, will give us an adrenaline rush and spread poison through our body.

In nature, animals automatically shake off their trauma. If you see a cat or dog bump into something or get hurt, they shake it off immediately. They shake their paw, or their leg, or their whole body wherever they feel pain. That is a natural healing response. Individual human beings may have forgotten how to do this, but it is part of our animal nature.

I'm here to remind you. Next time you watch the news and see some violence and all of a sudden feel horrible inside, I invite you to turn off the television, go into another room and literally shake it off. Think about those football players and how they jump up and shake themselves off after they take a big hit. They even shake their bodies before they start playing!

That's what I want you to do. Start shaking and shimmying your body. Shake it all over. Start with your bottom, then your legs and then your arms. Make believe that you're a funny dancer and do the shimmy. Don't be afraid of looking ridiculous, just do it! Make believe you're having fun. Let yourself feel really silly. Start laughing as you shake yourself loose.

Do this exercise with the intention of shaking all the trauma, all the sadness, all the hurt, all the grief out of your body. You will be surprised at how much better you will feel.

22: SHOP UNTIL HE DROPS?

My father was in the hospital, on his deathbed. He had taken a turn for the worse. I remember him tied down like some kind of wild animal trapped out in the woods. He looked so scared, so frightened of everything. He was fighting it. He did not want to die this way.

My mother said to the doctors on the ward, "Harry is not to be hooked up to these machines anymore; he did not want this. Unplug him!"

They said, "Where's the paper authorizing us to do that?"

My mother said, "His personal doctor has it." This was true.

The hospital doctors said, "Sorry, this is the weekend, and we can't get it until Monday. We have to keep your husband on life support until Monday."

My mother said, "I don't think so."

They said, "We can't do anything without the written authorization; there's nothing we can do about it." They gathered in a corner to talk and look at some charts. I noticed that Mamma had a strange look on her face.

She went over to Daddy and said, "Bye, Harry. I love you."

She pulled the plug when the doctors weren't looking.

Then she looked at me and said, "Let's go shopping."

I was in a trance, still trying to process what she had just done. I chose an alliance with my mother. We left my Daddy in the hospital to go shopping.

When I listened to Mamma, I became a child. My heart wanted to be with my father as he passed, but Mamma had pulled the plug, and she insisted we go shopping.

We went to Target. I remember feeling so uneasy about that shopping trip. Finally, when we got home, the hospital called. "Where were you?" they asked. "Your father passed away, one hour ago."

I had left my life in California rushed on a plane to be by my father's side when he passed away, only to go into some kind of childlike trance while listening to my mother. That's how Mamma got through things – she went shopping.

~~~~~~~~~~~~

HEALING MODALITY: LISTENING TO YOUR INNER VOICE

I was in my forties when my father passed away, but I became like a little girl, listening to my mother's voice more than my inner voice. I remember feeling extremely sad and disappointed that I had let my father die alone in a hospital bed without being there to comfort him. I was in great conflict. I had to do a lot of self-forgiveness to get over that one.

One day when I came home from work, I found my little girl, Gretchen, who was seven at the time, wearing a full leg cast.

Shocked, I asked her, "Sweetheart, what happened to you?"

"Jenny told me to jump down the stairs. She said we could fly."

I said, "Oh, she did, did she?" (Jenny was Gretchen's best friend and often her partner in crime. I was very curious to find out what had really happened. "Gretchen, do you remember our talk about the little voice inside you and how it speaks to you when you have choices in life?" She nodded yes.

I said, "Did you hear that little inner voice?"

"Yes, Mamma."

"Did it tell you it was okay for you to jump down the stairs?" I asked.

She said, "No, it said not to."

"Then why did you jump down the stairs?"

"Because Jenny's voice was yelling louder: *Jump. Jump. Jump!*"

I said, "But now, who's wearing the leg cast and can't go swimming or walk around all summer long? You or Jenny?"

Sadness settled over her little face. I said, "Next time something like that happens, whose voice are you going to listen to?"

"My inner voice," she said. It was sad, but it was a good lesson for her to learn so early.

~~~~~~~~~~~~

HEALING MODALITY: CONNECTING TO YOUR INNER VOICE

In previous chapters we have talked about centering, being still, and connecting to your own divinity. This exercise consolidates all of that work.

Set aside five to 30 minutes to do this and you will strengthen your connection to your own inner divinity and your own precious inner voice. Strengthen the muscle that makes this connection a daily reality, because that voice can literally save your life.

The world outside has a much louder voice, but you are the one who will reap the consequences if you listen to the noise instead of your own best guidance. On the other hand, you can receive great benefits of freedom and joy when you learn to connect and listen to your own inner voice.

Your inner voice will never tell you to harm yourself or harm anyone else. It will be the voice of self-love, self-care, compassion, kindness, wisdom and intelligence. It will tell you what's the highest and best for you at any given moment – so practice, practice, practice listening to it. It will bring progress, rewards, and miracles into your life.

Begin with the centering exercise I have shared earlier in this book. Breathe in love and light. Hold your breath for three seconds and then breathe out any and all thoughts and feelings connected to the past. Right now you are getting present. Hold the breath at the end for three seconds, and then breathe in the present moment. Hold it for three seconds and breathe out all future ideas, worries or concerns. Now breathe in the present moment. Breathe out and naturally allow yourself to become very still.

Now ask your internal counselor for guidance on any issue or question that is important to you ... and listen carefully for the answer of your inner voice. The answers will come when you are courageous enough to trust in the process.

23: "I WANT YOU NEXT TO ME"

It was December 2003. I got a phone message from my sister, Sue: "Dale, there's something wrong with Mamma. You've got to come home. Right away. It's urgent. Call me immediately. She is about to die."

Time stopped cold and broke into pieces. I had to put it back together by hand.

Three months earlier, I had started a two-year journey to earn my Masters degree in spiritual psychology. This was my third "long weekend" in that program, a period of intensive work, study, and self-analysis within a small group that was devoted to self-discovery and the healing of all the self-inflicted wounds I had accumulated over the years. I was there because I knew that I had been holding on to those wounds for many years; I was finally ready, I told myself, to look at my stories, to let them go, and to set myself free.

And then I got that phone message.

I became immediately angry and resentful at even the thought that my mother had decided to start dying now. How dare she interrupt me at this fateful time of my life, when I was on the verge, at long last, of healing myself from all the damage that she had inflicted on me! Maybe I wasn't quite as ready to set myself free as I thought.

Intellectually, I knew that was a foolish, immature response to an important moment in both of our lives, a response that did us both more harm than good. I certainly knew it was a step backwards for me. Yet, it was what I felt. I was in great conflict. I knew where I was really supposed to be that weekend; yet I did not want to go to see my mother. I still felt resentful. I flat-out didn't want to go, regardless of whether or not I was supposed to go.

Suddenly, memories of my mother began flooding through my mind, some of them difficult and painful. One of those memories kept surfacing and resurfacing: My mother saying to me, "Dale, when it's my time to die, I want you to be next to me."

> *"Dale, when it's my time to die, I want you to be next to me."*

As I returned to the class, it was obvious to everyone that I was upset. I raised my hand, and the instructor called on me.

I said, "I'm in terrible conflict. My mother is very sick, and I have a call saying she may not make it through the next few days. I don't want to see her. I don't think I'm ready. I can tell I'm still not healed."

A silence fell over the room, and then the instructor asked, "What would happen if you did not go and your mother died? How would you feel? Would you be okay with that?"

When I looked deep inside myself, I realized the answer was, "No, absolutely not."

I said goodbye to my classmates and began the journey home, praying all the way.

~~~~~~~~~~~~

HEALING MODALITY: RAISING YOUR VIBRATION

This exercise can be used first thing in the morning before you get out of bed, or whenever you find yourself slipping into negative thought patterns.

Everything in your world has a vibration and a frequency. Everything is energy. Now, if everything has an energy frequency, then your thoughts have energy, too. Your feelings have energy and vibrations ... so if you consciously put your thoughts and feelings into a higher vibration, you can have a higher quality of life.

Center yourself using the centering exercise. Now, remember a peak moment in your life when you felt really great. Maybe it was the first time you saw the ocean, or the first time you fell in love, or the time you got a new puppy. It's different for everyone. Pick something specific that you remember that made you very, very happy.

Re-create that joyous feeling; remember the taste of it, the sound of it, and the feel of it. Breathe it in and keep remembering this feeling for three to six seconds, and then, from that place, imagine how you want the rest of your life to be. Now that you have brought your vibration to a very high frequency, one of celebration, joy and happiness, imagine what it is that you want to create.

It could be finishing that creative project. Imagine it already finished. See yourself celebrating your success with friends, family and peers. Imagine the colors, the smells, and the sounds. Or it could be the completion of your work at school. See yourself on stage receiving your diploma; hear friends and family cheering for you. Imagine looking at the photograph of your graduation with a big smile on your face with all your loved ones around you. It could be that you see yourself in a marathon, crossing the finish line with a big grin on your face. It could be a financial goal; see your ATM screen with a balance of $100,000 or $1,000,000. It could be your dream home; see yourself walking through it, admiring your lovely new living space. It could be the perfect relationship; imagine yourself with your beloved, hand-in-hand, walking on the beach, in the mountains, or having a nice dinner together.

You get the idea. Use this exercise to visualize events that will bring you even more happiness. Whatever it is you want to create in your life, you have the power to create it in your own mind first. Elevate yourself to the celebratory vibration of having already accomplished what you want. Enjoy it now!

24: NOT READY YET

I was in constant prayer throughout the journey home to be with my mother, and much of the prayer was fueled by the inspiring music that I slid into my CD player. Music and prayer were what kept me from slipping into darkness.

As it turned out, my mother had two and a half weeks before she passed away. But I didn't know that the first time I saw her in bed. She was very weak. She told me she hadn't eaten in the last few days; that her throat was closing up.

Mamma had a morphine drip and a woman from hospice who helped her around the clock. I don't know how we would have gotten through that time without the help of the women of Elizabeth Hospice, who spent countless hours in my mother's home, caring for her. They were grace in human form.

Every day, I was by Mamma's side from eight in the morning until nine at night. Whenever I did leave, I lived only 10 minutes away. If they needed me, I told the hospice workers, I would be there, any time.

It was hard to be there every day like that, but the decision to stay by my mother's side led to something beautiful. To understand what it was, you have to understand that I had hated this woman for most of my life and had prayed many times for her to die. I had stayed away from her for years before we reconciled. I had experienced all those wounds; had blamed her often for my troubles, issues, problems, and pain.

But now, sitting next to her, I got to put that all aside and remember why I had forgiven her I got to embrace her, sing to her, pray for her, love her, and be her spiritual midwife to the next world. It was a transformative experience.

My sister Sue and I witnessed some very interesting phenomena during the last two and a half weeks of our mother's life. In the very beginning, the side door to her house was always kept open; she seemed to prefer being able to look outside. One time, though, while she was staring at that open door, Mamma got a strange look on her face. It seemed like she was looking at something by the door, something that Sue and I could not see.

Mamma was as Italian as you can get, and she had always used her hands to express how she felt about things. In this moment, as she looked out through the doorway, she made a very powerful hand gesture; thumb up, as if she were indicating kicking someone out of the room. She meant business. As she made that movement, she shouted, "Get out! I said get out! I'm not ready yet!"

Sue and I were perplexed. We asked Mamma whom she was talking to.

She replied, with strong determination, "That was the Angel of Death. He's coming to get me, but I'm not ready yet." Then she asked us to close the door to "keep him out."

~~~~~~~~~~~~~~

HEALING MODALITY: RELEASING NEGATIVITY

When you're not feeling like yourself, when you're depressed or down on yourself, you are likely to have negative feelings, thinking, and self-talk. (Self-talk is the constant chatter in your brain.) When you can remember to be aware and say, "Wait a minute! This is not who I am," you are waking up. This will happen more often as you recover from Mamma Trauma. You will begin to realize when the negative self-talk is there. You will begin to become more mindful of your own thinking. This is what you want.

Some people call negative self-talk "stinkin' thinkin'." I think it's a good idea to put a humorous slant to the process of noticing how you think.

When you notice yourself falling into negative self-talk, call upon your angels and connect to your own Divinity. Name the issues that appear to be driving the negativity – whether it's grief, anger, fear, feeling unworthy, or any form of exaggerated self-criticism. Once you have identified the particular negative thinking you have been engaging in, say this prayer.

Prayer for Releasing Negativity

"As I connect to my own Divinity right now, which is Love, Light and Peace, I command you (insert negative emotions here) to be pulled away from my body, mind, and spirit right now. I send you to the sun NOW! Go back to the light to

become beneficial energy, away from my body, mind, and spirit now! Go back to the sun. You have no power over me anymore! I am taking charge of myself and I choose love, peace and freedom, harmony, laughter, joy and health. Thank you Source! Thank you, God. Thank you Divine Intelligence. So it is. So be it. Amen. It is done!"

Here is sweet little powerful prayer that has helped hundreds of thousands of people get through tough times. I invite you to memorize it and draw on it when you need strength or find yourself falling into "stinkin' thinkin"!

God grant me the serenity to accept the things I cannot change; courage to change the things I can; and wisdom to know the difference. Amen.

(Part of the Serenity Prayer from Alcoholics Anonymous)

Replace, Affirm and Restore to Happiness

And now it's time to find some great, uplifting music that carries powerful positive affirmations. Take the time to listen to that music right away. If you can, go on a nature walk so you can experience the healing force of nature as you listen to the music that makes your soul soar. Or you can put the music on and dance. The right music can anchor you in the Truth of your being, and re-frame your whole existence within that Truth, reminding you that you are joy, love, peace, happiness, wisdom, health, balance and freedom.

Music is a very important tool. I suggest that you use it often, especially after releasing negativity to replace it with positive energy. However, it is extremely important that you expose yourself only to songs that have positive affirmations, with uplifting words and music. Make sure to listen to these kinds of songs often, and avoid music that makes you feel worse. The right music will help guide your self-talk back to happiness.

My favorite music right now comes from Agape International Choir, Rickie Byers Beckwith, and all songs by Karen Drucker. These are life affirming, uplifting songs. They can help you change your subconscious patterns, change your perception, change your thoughts, feelings and behavior, and change your life so that you are refocusing more quickly and easily on your own highest and best good.

25: SONGS MY MAMMA SANG

By the time I watched my mother shoo off the Angel of Death, I had realized that making the choice to be with her during her final days had been the right one. In just a little over a week, I had grown a lot as a person.

It had taken every bit of strength I had to decide to walk into my mother's house and spend time with her as she died. The moment I opened the door, I saw my sister Sue. We fell into each other's arms and wept like babies. We held each other for a long time; and we got very close. In fact, the more time we spent with each other, the stronger we became. I was so glad to have her there for support, and I could tell that she felt the same way. The days of anger and hatred and recrimination between us felt very far away indeed.

"Her joy and her zest for life came through her as she whisper-sang those songs into the microphone."

Now, a week or so into the vigil, we were side-by-side at our mother's deathbed. Sue sat on one side of Mamma and I sat on the other. We did our best to surround her with love, singing her love songs and lullabies we had learned as we were mothering our own children. My mother had never sung those kinds of songs to us, but we figured, why not sing her the songs that we, as children, had longed to hear her sing to us? So we did. We could tell she enjoyed them.

As it happened, Mamma's neighbor was a professional singer, fortuitously named Frankie, who sang just like Frank Sinatra. He loved singing the old songs, and he was quite the entertainer. He was in his 70s, and he was very fond of my mother. We asked him if he would give her a private concert and he agreed. This was very special, because Mamma loved to sing when she was younger, and had had ambitions of becoming a professional singer. She used to tell us stories of the nightclubs and the agents and how her dad would not allow her to follow her dream. So that was a part of her that she never got to fully express.

However, when Frankie came over with all of his equipment and started singing her songs from her past, she lit up like a Christmas tree. She was so happy; she could hardly contain herself. Even in her weakened state, she somehow found the strength to sing (or at least whisper) along with Frankie. Then she asked for the microphone. We could hardly hear any sound come from her voice, but the energy of the song was so beautiful and so clear that it went right to our hearts. "New York, New York." "I Left My Heart in San Francisco." On and on. Her joy and her zest for life came through her as she whisper-sang those songs into the microphone. I recorded them. They still make me cry whenever I listen to them. She really was a star after all.

174

~~~~~~~~~~~~~

HEALING MODALITY: DON'T DIE WITH YOUR SONG UNSUNG

Is there some part of you, deep, inside, that has a creative urge waiting to be expressed? Something buried deep down – a childhood dream, perhaps? A song that you need to sing or compose? A dance that you need to dance? A painting that you need to paint? A book you need to write? An instrument you need to learn to play? So ... why haven't you? What's holding you back?

Everyone is creative. Some of us make choices on the way to adulthood that inhibit our creativity. We learn to think, "I'm not that good an artist," or "I can't sing that well," or "The way I paint looks ridiculous." We judge ourselves and stop the flow of creativity in our lives. When we do this, we may sabotage, or even kill, an important part of ourselves, a very precious, beautiful part of our unique human expression.

I suggest that you find a way to reconnect with your creative self. You can do this by spending a little time in nature – at the forest, the beach, or the lake – or simply by getting very still and listening very attentively during one or more of your meditations. Think about doing the bedtime meditation from Chapter Five, and channeling the results toward something creative. Don't let your creative self die without expression. You made choices along the way. You can continue to make choices. Choose to create something that is uniquely you, a personal expression of your own being.

Find a way to center yourself and ask the question, "If I have all the money in the world, all the time in the world, all the freedom in the world, and I had only one year to live, what would I do?" Write down your answers on a clean piece of paper – ideally, without relying too much on your logical mind. Take off your judgment hat and just write down all the people you want to meet, all the things that you want to do, all the places you want to go, and all the things you want to have. What is it that you really want to be or do ... and how?

Allow yourself to write all this down quickly. Give yourself at least 20 minutes with this question. This will get to the very essence of what your heart wants to do. The wisest among us learn to listen to our own heart and follow our own bliss. What do you have to lose? Be one of those wise people for twenty minutes ... and listen to what your heart tells you to do in the realm of creative action and expression.

26: CRYBABY, CRY

One afternoon, Sue and I heard the hospice nurse say to my mother, "Kitty, we need to take your teeth out now. They're too big for your mouth. Your mouth has shriveled up, and it's dangerous to leave your teeth in."

My sister and I looked at each other simultaneously with the same expression and the same silent question: *What?*

We looked back at Mamma and saw that terror had taken over her face. Her fear had something to do with the inevitability of her own death. With this demand from the hospice nurse, my mother got it. It had finally sunk in. This was serious. This was the endgame. No matter what she said to that nurse, her teeth would have to go soon, the last remnants of her former appearance would have to go soon. Sue and I could tell that a chunk of her ego would be going, too — but not without a fight.

> *"As bizarre as the joke was, it brought us closer together, and it allowed me to look at her face and see the love she had for me."*

Mamma had always had a fighting, feisty part of her character. That stayed with her, right until the end. And we

177

saw it that afternoon. She shook her head and pulled all the strength she had inside of her to say out loud, a strong and very clear sentence: "No! Not my teeth!"

At that stage, it was a pretty big deal to hear her say a sentence that clearly.

She gave it a good fight, but finally, when she had no more strength left to fight with, she relented. The next day, she gave in. Out came the dentures and her ego collapsed.

I admit it. This is the point at which I lost it. I ran to the kitchen (where Mamma couldn't see me) and thrust my head over the sink. A wave of nausea moved through my body, and I thought for sure that I was going to throw up. I held onto the sink; a gut-wrenching sob caught hold of me and fought its way out. I had never seen my mother without her teeth. There was nothing hypothetical about it anymore. She was really going to die. She had threatened to die many times, and had come very close to death, but never this close, never so close that there was no going back. This was definitely the end.

It took about five minutes for me to recover. I washed my face. My eyes were bright red and swollen almost shut, but I mustered up as much courage as I could find and made my way back into Mamma's room. She took one look at me, released that old, familiar, wicked laugh, and with fiery, glowing eyes, stared me down and said in her husky voice, "Crybaby!"

It was oddly comforting. I thought of all the times she had told me when I was a child, "Stop your crying, or I'll give me something to cry about." There were countless times that she had actually given me something to cry about. I had eventually learned to never cry in her presence. And now, here she was, making some strange, twisted joke about it all. As bizarre as the joke was, it brought us closer together, and it allowed me to look at her face and see the love she had for me.

~~~~~~~~~~~~

HEALING MODALITY: FEEL YOUR FEELINGS AND EXPRESS THEM

People literally get sick from pushing their emotions down into their body, rather than expressing them. Emotions are our guidance system. They let us know when things are right for us and not right for us. Sometimes we feel emotions like sadness, grief, fear, depression, frustration, or unworthiness, and if we don't acknowledge these emotions and let them out, they can end up hurting us from the inside out. These emotions can be expressed by writing them out, by talking them through, or even by sitting down and having a good cry.

Here are two healing exercises to help you access and release these deep emotions.

For immediate, strong emotions like grief and sadness:

Excuse yourself, go to the bathroom, get a towel so you can express full tears and sound into the towel (or inside of your arm) and wail like a little baby – let it come out! If you only have a certain amount time – say, five minutes, allow yourself that time. If there's still more emotion, tell yourself you'll come back and deal with it at a later time. Make sure you do that within 30 days.

The important thing is to feel it as fully as you possibly can in the moment. Grief can be a special challenge, because it sometimes sweeps through your entire body like a tidal wave. When it hits you really hard, just get on the floor like a baby and cry fully for 5 minutes (like a child in a fetal ball), and then get up, wash your face with cold water and go outside. Change your state. To help you let go of the past moment, situation, or circumstance, take physical action (a walk or a shower, for example). Say, "I release this pain." Take a breath in and blow it out three times, breathing in light and love and breathing out the pain: "pushed down" emotions, like frustration, sadness, depression, unworthiness, fear, and disappointment.

Light a candle and say a prayer of protection. Imagine a golden bubble of light all around you. You are in the center of the bubble. Say a prayer of protection.

Prayer of Protection

I am always safe, divinely guided, directed and protected by my higher power (or whichever deity you use). I am one with love and light. Thank you, I know this is true as I accept this as so. My heart is filled with gratitude. I release this to the LAW. I am safe and so it is! (Follow this with the centering prayer, if you have time.)

Here's another approach. Take a piece of paper. Fold it in half lengthwise. On the left side, write down "I love myself just the way I am." On the right side, write down what your critical mind is saying back to you. For example, "You're a crybaby." "You're weak." As things come up, feel your feelings and allow yourself to cry.

Give yourself 20 minutes maximum for this exercise. When you're done, rip up the paper, or safely burn it, and as you're doing that know that you're letting the pain go, giving it to your Higher Power (or the deity of your choice) and ask to be healed.

Then change your state of consciousness. Again, changing your state means taking a physical action to let go of the past moment, situation, or circumstance.

HEALING MODALITY: MERGING EXERCISE

Make believe you are five years old, that wonderful time in life when you can imagine anything to be real. Go and look at a bird and make believe that you merge with that bird. That's right. Make believe, as a child would, pretend that you are one with the bird. When it flies, imagine that you are the bird flying. Feel the air under your wings. Fly high and let yourself be lifted by the wind. Imagine feeling the great freedom and exaltation of flight, look down at the earth and see how small everything really is. Then fly your way right through any feeling that once seemed huge and impossible to navigate.

Don't be the walking dead, the people who are dying in their bodies before they ever really live. Get yourself into the world of being free to feel your own feelings. Play like a child; be open to experience all of life, all the pain, all the joy, all the tears, and all the laughter. Live your life fully and in color. Express yourself!

27: A VIEW TO THE OTHER SIDE

The fact that Mamma was not only facing death, but actually ready to die, was enough of a reason for my sister Sue and I to have a good stiff drink together.

We downed half of a big bottle of vodka in one sitting. I drank the vodka straight; my sister needed orange juice. (*What a sissy,* I muttered under my breath as she made her screwdriver. She just smiled.)

We had never done anything like that before, and we never did anything like it again. We had both wanted to stay sober for the entire event, and, outside of this one sisterly binge, that's what we did. This one time, though, we did drink, and we toasted to love, and to healing, to forgiveness, and to Mamma. The unlikely communion over alcohol made both of us feel a little better; but even after half a bottle of vodka, the reality of Mamma's imminent death did not allow us to get *really* drunk.

About eight days before Mamma actually passed, we had the whole family – well, most of the family, along with a few close friends – come over to Mamma's home and say their goodbyes around her deathbed. It was a difficult moment, but beautiful in its own unique way.

Shortly after that, when it was clear to all of us that she was ready to go, Mamma asked us to open the door to "let him in and tell him that I'm ready."

There was a great silence while we all let that one sink in. Then I opened the door, presumably to allow the Angel of Death easier access to my mother.

For the rest of the time we had with her, Mamma mostly lay quietly, matter-of-factly, nonchalant, watching the room or watching us. Once in a while, she would say something like, "Oh, there is my mother," or "Oh, there is my father." Or: "Oh, there is my mother-in-law, she's telling me to stop fighting; she's telling me it is okay to go." She talked about many people on the other side that came to visit her, to invite her to join them.

The most unusual part of this experience was not that she saw people from the other side, but that Mamma had no emotion in her voice as she described these people. Her voice was flat, and there was no emotion from her at all in the final days of her life. Perhaps all of her emotional energy was all used up. Or perhaps she had learned something about emotion. In any event, this was different. Throughout her earlier life, Mamma had been one heck of a firecracker; always driven by her feelings, through a somewhat fractured emotional body. As she died, however, she showed me another side, a side I was not used to seeing from her: acceptance.

~~~~~~~~~~~~

HEALING MODALITY: SURRENDER TO THE LIGHT

Here is a <u>healing prayer</u> for the times that try our souls.

I light this candle to connect with my Divinity. I ask _____ [my angels, guides and teachers; for me it is Jesus Christ and the Holy Spirit] to assist me in doing my inner work. I know there is only one power, one Light. I am one with Light now. As the wave surrenders to the ocean, I surrender to God within and to God who runs the universe, to the power and presence of Love that is the glue that holds the universe together. I release all fear, all worries, all doubts; all thoughts that I can't do it, all saboteurs, all parts of me that have not come to the Light yet. I now surrender you to the Light.

As I look at this candle, it represents that I am surrendered to the Light. I ask for courage. I ask for the courage to let go of what no longer serves me, the courage to open up, to accept and receive the love, the nurturing, and the connection to another person. I ask that my inner child be very present with me and my adult self has the courage to ask for what I need.

And so I know that as I ask, I am open to a deeper place of loving. I know that God is good and the universe is for me not against me. I re-establish my belief in a loving, powerful God and let go of the old beliefs of a punishing God. I open up and allow myself to receive the belief that I am worthy of the very best that Love and Light have to offer.

I ask for the courage to be able to ask for what I need. My little child joins me and I do it in a playful, loving, fun way. I ask for the courage to have eye contact so I can truly connect to another.

Knowing that the universe always says "YES!" God always says, "Yes" to Love! I now release this prayer with conviction of the law of manifestation. I let it go and I say "thank you!" As I let it go, I celebrate and know that what I ask always comes back to me fulfilled. My prayer is fulfilled. So I say, "Yes!" "Thank you!" I release this word. I simply allow it to be. I now fully and completely accept it on all levels. Thank you, God! Thank you, Universe! Thank you, Love! And so it is. Amen. So it is done.

(Note: The prerequisite for the exercise that follows is a connection with your inner child.) Now that you have courageously said your prayer, think about someone whom you trust, someone with whom you feel very safe. It could be a good friend, a sister, a brother, or even, if you have loved and healed enough, your own mother.

You will need to get back in touch with the little boy or little girl inside of yourself (usually between two and seven years old, maybe up to nine). Ask whether she/he is willing to play this game with you ... If the answer is "yes," you are ready to move on.

Recall that you have previously found a safe grownup person with whom you can do this exercise. Go to that person (you should be at their home, or in a place where you can feel safe and comfortable and be guaranteed uninterrupted quiet time) and ask whether he or she will assist you in this healing exercise. Explain that he or she will need to be totally supportive and loving to you.

If the person is willing, begin by connecting with your inner child and playfully asking, "I need five minutes to play a little game, okay?" Ask this in a fun, playful way. Let your little child come out. Make eye contact as a child would; let your body move as a little child would move.

Set a timer for five minutes and no more. Make a mental note that this is not a time for deep therapy, deep crying, or deep releasing. It really is just a game.

Take the person's hand and gently lead him or her to a couch. Put your head in the person's lap, and say, "I need my Mamma now." Ask the person to stroke your head and play this little game with you. In the game, they need to be the most nurturing, loving mother possible. That means they would stroke your head, look lovingly at you and gently say, "It's okay. I'm listening."

Now this is the time when you get to say whatever you feel like saying. You could say things like, "I'm really hurt." Or: "I feel bad." Or: "No one likes me." Or: "I miss my puppy." Just let yourself be fully expressive of your feelings. It doesn't have to be deep or dramatic. Start with the little stuff.

During this game, just allow yourself to be nurtured and lovingly touched. Let the person stroke your head, your arms or your shoulders in a loving, nurturing way. After the time is up, sit up, smile and give your assistant a big hug. Say thank you, giggle, and go your way.

28: THE LAST SHOPPING DAY

The last month of my mother's life, we went shopping at Costco.

I remember she rode down the aisles in an automatic wheelchair. She had resisted the wheelchair for many years and this was the first time she took it for a ride. She seemed totally in control as she rolled down the aisles, gleeful and engaged. It was beautiful, the way people looked at us when we were shopping together. It was particularly beautiful on that last shopping trip at Costco.

I like to think my mother was at her happiest when she was shopping with her daughters. It didn't matter what we were shopping for: hot dogs, bubbles for my wedding, clothes, and crystals. She was just proud to have her beautiful daughters next to her.

> *"Our connection was finally more powerful than the decades of painful separation."*

On this day, she was very happy to realize that her daughter wanted to spend time with her. People would look at us and a full smile of compassion would spread across their faces. It was like their hearts opened up to see an elderly mother with her daughter, like a new mother with her baby child.

Something is beautiful about the beginning of life, and something is beautiful about the end of life. That something, whatever it is, brings tenderness to the center of our being.

Every chance I got, I held Mamma's hands, and felt the tenderness in the love and the compassion that we'd finally found. After all the hurts and all the pain and all the forgiveness, there was now only love. Our hearts melted into one heart as we wandered through the aisles.

Finally, we had arrived. The love we felt for each other was more present than the resentment. Our connection was finally more powerful than the decades of painful separation.

HEALING MODALITY: TOUCH

When my Mamma's fragile hands were in mine, I felt
compassion and forgiveness on the cellular level and felt a
warm melting of the vast, icy pain of past injuries. Our love
was real, experienced, touched, and felt.

"To touch can be to give life," said Michelangelo. He was
absolutely right. We live in a high-tech, low-touch society. We
are more isolated than ever before. It is time to reach out and
connect with the ones we love, time to touch and be touched.

The power of touch is deep. It has been said that our
hands are extensions of our hearts. The more we open our
hearts and connect, the healthier and happier we become.

I was twenty-four years old when I was hugged by my first
spiritual teacher, Katherine Hayward, and I still remember
how my body stiffened and I felt scared to death. I wasn't used
to platonic touches. The only kind of friendly touch that I was
familiar with was sexual. Loving hugs and touches were very
rare in my family.

Many of us didn't have tender loving touches as children –
or if we did, we find we now live in a world where the tender
touch is often not a priority. Loving touches can be scary at
first if we haven't experienced them for a long time or are not
used to them. So if it is scary to you to touch or be touched,
start by going slow. When you shake someone's hand wrap
both your hands around their hand with the intention of really
connecting with that person. Look into his or her eyes and

191

really connect. Or give someone a pat on the arm, or a squeeze of the shoulder.

Ask for hugs from friends and family. Offer hugs, too. Resist the urge to tell people that you aren't the "hugging type". Allow yourself to be fully present to receive and give a hug. When you give a hug, make sure you put your head to the others person's left; that way you connect heart-to-heart. Take in a deep breath and feel the person in your arms, really feel them and allow yourself to be felt. Experiment and feel the difference between one person's hug and another person's. Let the person know that you are connecting heart-to-heart. Most people really like that idea.

Touch has been scientifically proven to activate compassion, safety, trust and wellbeing, by releasing oxytocin. Oxytocin has been called the "love hormone" because it works as an anti-stress chemical. It has a soothing, healing effect on us. It helps us to heal from trauma, to feel secure and loved.

I invite you to do an experiment for one month. See how many things on the following list you can do, and see whether doing them makes a difference in the way you feel about yourself and others. At the end of each day, see whether you can check off at least three items on this list. Please add to this list if you come up with other ways to touch and be touched that are healthy and feel good. At the end of 30 days evaluate and see if you feel happier and have a higher state of well-being.

- Pet a dog or cat

- Dance

- Hold hands

- Hug or cuddle

- Make love

- Volunteer and be of service, give to others who need your helping touch (for instance, assisted living or convalescent homes)

- Pray while holding the hands of another person

- Get a massage, or do some energy work (such as Reiki) where you are touched

29: MAMMA'S THREE LAST WORDS

Mamma had been at her home, and I had been helping to take care of her, for about three weeks, when my mind gave way.

She was in her bed. I stood there, watching her, and it felt to me like she was sleeping. So much time, effort, attention, and energy had gone into me being there for her, looking mature, feeling mature, and acting mature.

I was quite proud of my maturity and personal growth. I had actually convinced myself that I was finally beyond the pain and the heartache of our long past together.

But all of a sudden, the floodgates burst.

Sharp, painful thoughts came hurtling around every corner of my mind. I was unprepared for their intensity. I felt this bizarre, massive wave of negativity toward her. I couldn't stop the loud thoughts:

Come on, Mamma, when are you going to die? For God's sake, here I am sitting next to you for over three weeks. I have been here a long time already. Is this going to last forever?

This is just like you to be selfish and make me wait here this long, when we both know what happens next. When are you going to die already? I am a busy person. I have things to do, places to go to, and people to see!

It was childish, and to this day I don't know where it came from. All I know is that a tidal wave of anger, disgust and impatience had picked up the little ship of my consciousness, and was throwing it from side to side.

Then the strangest thing happened. Now mind you, I am willing to swear under oath that I never said one word of these horrible thoughts out loud. Yet in the next instant, Mamma opened her eyes, looked straight into mine, and spoke her very last words to me.

"Patience, Dale, patience."

*****

Three days later, I was leaning close to her, whispering into her ear: "Your son George is not coming. He's on his way, but it's going to be too late. He called and he wants me to let you know that it's okay to go. He forgives you; he loves you. We all forgive you, Mamma. It's okay now. You're free to go. We forgive you. We love you. We love you, Mamma."
And her breathing changed at that moment.

> *"Patience, Dale, patience."*

A few hours after that, she moved her head from the tilt of the right to the tilt of the left, her eyes opened, and there was one big gasp of air.

The hospice worker said, "She's gone."

~~~~~~~~~~~~~

HEALING MODALITY: PATIENCE/NO MISTAKE

What is patience anyway? Patience means being fully present in the moment. It means not looking at what's going to happen in the next minute, where you have to go, what you have to do. It means completely surrendering to be present in this moment. It means letting go of all judgments of where I should be and where I shouldn't be.

When I surrender to the moment I feel peace. And I trust this moment is everything I need. Patience is a quality of spirit that was given to me at birth, but it was blocked by stress and trauma that disconnected me from the essence of who I am. I have had to learn how to heal myself from the blocks in order to be patient again. I learned I cannot be egocentric and patient at the same time.

Being patient is being supportive. I have to know that I am supported first, so I can support others. I have learned that by doing the exercises that I have given you in this book, I have supported myself enough now to be patient, to be present, to be loving and kind to myself first. Now I am capable to embrace the quality of patience with deep and sincere gratitude. So thank you, Mamma, for giving me this precious gift of awareness that patience is one of the highest human qualities; a gift that I have now accepted as my own.

How do find your patience? By doing the exercises in this book, by removing the blocks that keep you from your essence, by building yourself a strong conscious connection with your own divinity in the center of your own heart ... and learning to trust and know that all your needs are met, now and always. If you trust, that means you know you are supported and that you are in the right place at the right time, doing just what you need to do.

Remember to connect to your own Divinity and ask for help every day, first thing in the morning, for spiritual guidance, emotional strength and a healthy body, mind and spirit. At the end of every day, say thank you, thank you, thank you and count your blessings instead of sheep. Know that all is well.

Here's my final word on patience: When teaching yoga to my daughter's kindergarten class, I taught them how to put their hands together in a prayer position in front of their heart, to look into another person's eyes and say, "Namaste." I said, "'Namaste' means that the love in my heart says 'hello' to the love in your heart." At the end of the class, a proud little boy, named Miguel, came to me with his hands together in prayer position, looked straight into my eyes, and said, "No Mistake." How right he was! My first spiritual teacher, Katherine Hayward, told me that we never make a mistake and that there are no mistakes. Everything that we do has a benefit and has a lesson for us to learn, grow strong, and if we choose to, be a beneficial presence on our planet. So know with every part of your body, mind and spirit, that there are no mistakes. So be gentle, be kind and have patience for yourself.

30: EPILOGUE

One of the proudest days of my life was after I completed my Masters program and graduated from the University of Santa Monica's Spiritual Psychology program. Not long after the graduation, the graduates had a reunion. As part of the gathering, I was sitting in what is known as "the client chair". We engaged in a small group healing process where I played the role of the client. This is when I realized that I really had graduated, that the miracle of healing had finally taken place in my life.

The exercise was around inner child work. I asked, "How are you little Dale?" I was amazed by the response. My eight-year-old inner child showed up and was radiantly beautiful and happy. She was at peace. Her name had changed from Rambo to Rainbow. Rainbow felt joy and was light inside her heart. Rainbow is my feminine energy, expressed with playfulness, innocence, beauty and grace.

In the past, it was Rambo who would show up. Rambo was dressed in camouflage pants and shirts. She had a machine gun in her hand. She wore swords and knives on her belt. She had matted hair and dirty fingernails. Anger and hatred were in her eyes. Her mission was to destroy. Her purpose was to make others hurt the way she hurt.

I asked, "Where is Rambo?" Rainbow replied, "Rambo is here for you any time. But just for fun."

Rainbow likes me to bring her to the ocean. We jump in, look for the dolphins and swim with the dolphins. She also likes to dance like a ballerina on stage. I am her biggest fan. I tell her she's beautiful. She's the biggest love in my whole life. She's unique and special and no one is like her. In return she gives me creativity, joy, light, laughter, and endless energy. We actually boogie board together!

I had been working on healing my inner child consciously for the past 40 years. This is the payoff: Rambo has finally become Rainbow!

I am filled with gratitude and great appreciation for every part of every experience I have encountered on my journey. I never thought the day would come when I would experience balance, joy, freedom and great gratitude on a daily basis. But that day has come for me. And it can for you, too.

I am here to offer you support for any healing you may need. My journey helped me recover from Mamma Trauma and thrive in a life that I now love. I know that your journey can do the same for you. But you must make the choice to make the journey for yourself! No one else can walk it for you.

~~~~~~~~~~~~

HEALING MODALITY: Choose!

An elderly Cherokee Indian was teaching his grandchildren about life. They asked many questions, but one was really important.

They asked him, "Why do you seem so happy when we know you have been through such hard times?"

He said to them, "A fight is going on inside of me. It is a terrible fight, and it is between two wolves:

One wolf represents fear, anger, envy, sorrow, regret, greed, arrogance, self-pity, guilt, loneliness, resentment, inferiority, lies, false pride, superiority and ego.

The other wolf stands for joy, peace, love, gratitude, hope, sharing, serenity, humility, kindness, benevolence, friendship, empathy, generosity, truth, compassion, and faith.

This same fight is going on inside you, and inside every other person."

The grandchildren thought about it for a minute and then one child asked his grandfather, "Which wolf will win?"

The old Cherokee simply replied, "The one you feed."

Which wolf are you feeding today...simply put...the one of love or fear?

It's your choice.

31: THE POWER OF PRAYER

Prayer has saved my life many times. And because I know it can save yours, too, I have added this chapter.

I start each day with prayer. I pray throughout the day. I end each day with prayer. My favorite prayer is that of deep sincere gratitude from my heart for all that is good, for the countless blessings I have received in this amazing life. I say a prayer of thanks for the privilege of living and sharing life with others.

The immense power of prayer has been the subject of literally thousands of books. Prayer is not superstition. Prayer works. There is now ample scientific evidence proving this blessed truth ... but that's not what I want to share with you here. I want to talk to you on a very personal level about the untapped power of praying to God. When I use the word "God" in prayer, I am appealing to the Divine in a devotional way. When I use the words "Divine Intelligence" and "Source" in prayer, the prayer comes in me and through me as me, making me an expression of God. I will share more with you about this distinction in a moment.

WHY PRAY?

Prayer is uttered from millions of mouths and hearts every day. Why?

I believe the answer is to be found in the indisputable fact that everything is energy, and in the practical reality that human beings are drawn to energy. I believe the law of the Universe always says yes to focused attention, intention, directing your will with the highest will of the Loving Intelligence that guides and directs the universe, also known as God. Why do this? Something in you already knows the answer to that.

It is my belief that all prayer is good as long as we pray for a loving outcome, for the highest and best outcome for someone or something.

TWO KINDS OF PRAYER

As I see it, there are two different kinds of prayer. I use both of them.

The first kind is devotional prayer. Coming from a Catholic background as I do, I used to pray to God, figuratively speaking to someone who had a long white beard and was in a big throne up there in Heaven somewhere. I used to believe that God was like Superman, and would sometimes punish me when I'd been bad, or reward me when I was good. I used to pray and barter with God. I would say, "God, if I'm a good girl would you give me this?" When I was hurt, I knew it was because I'd been a very bad girl and deserved to be punished; God was punishing me. I knew that, because my mother told me that that was true. I have given prayer a lot of thought and changed my mind since then. I changed my concept of God and the Divine Intelligence. However there are still some parts of that little girl within me that likes to pray to some masculine Divine energy believing He will always take care of me. I consider this a form of devotional prayer.

There is absolutely nothing wrong with devotional prayer. All prayer works! I believe we do have a loving God who finds a way to say "yes" to everyone who has a strong intention and desire and who asks for help from above. I believe there is a benevolent loving Source of all energy that always says "yes", and I believe that appealing to that Source through devotional prayer can bring great blessings.

I call the other kind of prayer scientific prayer. This is the kind of prayer that I use more now than anything else. I learned this prayer from my very first spiritual science of mind mentor and teacher, Kathryn Hayward, when I was 23 years old. This scientific prayer is simply an intention mixed with the emotions and feelings of the heart in connection to Divine Intelligence and then speaking it AS IF it were the present reality.

When we mix the energy of strong feelings and emotion with our own clarified and focused thoughts, when we speak from the heart the words that match what we want in our lives, when we do that with the image and the conviction that it has already taken place, this is what I call Declaration. Declaration is commanding Something from the unseen-world into the physical-world reality. I believe there is great power in Declaration.

Such powerful prayers come from a place of connecting to the Divine, to God, to the loving Source that runs the universe, to Divine Intelligence, and then speaking from the heart exactly what you are ready to accept. For instance, you might be ready to accept qualities of peace, joy, love, harmony, freedom, radiant health, beauty, abundance, prosperity, Divine right action, or all of the above.

I like to end all my prayers with a Declaration for the highest and best good for all.

In scientific prayer, I declare what I am focusing my attention on AS IF it has already manifested, and feel its existence in my heart and my bones with full conviction. I am confirming the factuality of the images in my mind, as one would confirm a scientific proof. I am moving from believing to knowing.

This prayer is essentially the same as imagination ... but it is a special kind of imagination. It is imagination that has been infused with the power of Infinite Intelligence. Sometimes people pray this way without even realizing that that's what they're doing.

I believe one of the most beautiful scientific prayers of our time appears in a song by John Lennon: Do you remember? He challenged each us to imagine all the people in the world living lives of peace.

Why not imagine? Why not pray for peace, harmony, love, freedom, abundance, health? Why not imagine and pray for peace and for a world that works for everyone? I would love it if you would join me in that prayer. Imagine this is my invitation for you. Of course, you could say that I'm just another dreamer. But Lennon knew that dreamers who band together have the power to change the world.

At any time you choose, you can use prayer to change your own world, and the world we all live in, for the better. After you claim the qualities of what you are ready to accept - what you really want - and you imagine it to be so, speak it AS IF it already is, then feel it in your heart. As you do this you release your Declaration to the Divine.

And this I do on your behalf now, because as you read these words, you are at this very moment experiencing and actualizing the limitless power of prayer in your own life. Thank you Source, I release this to the law, and so it is. Amen. I know it is done. So be it.

Dale Bach

P.S. As a gift to everyone who has read my book and would like to receive a free MP3 recording of me sharing the Centering Prayer from chapter one, please use this special link to my website:

www.DaleBach.com/mamma-trauma.html

Centering Prayer (Ch.1)

[Heavenly Father. Divine Mother. Holy Spirit, legions of angels connected to the Highest Source of Love and Light.] I surrender to you now anything and everything that has kept me separate from realizing my oneness with you. I open up and ask to be guided by you and to be shown clearly the way that is for my highest good. I surrender all fears, all pain of the past, all judgments, all blame. I give it to you. I don't want it anymore. I empty myself now and am filled with the divine light, love and wisdom of my true authentic self. It is from this place of oneness that I claim and know that I am a divine emanation of the Most High.

That peace that passes human understanding is my birthright. Beauty is my divine essence. Joy is the truth of my soul. I connect to this and I allow myself to be set free knowing this truth. Guide me and allow me to heal those places inside of myself that still hurt.

Elevate my perception so I may really be able to see the truth that will set me free. Please help me go beyond blame and shame so that I may find my wholeness once again.

Thank you for this. Thank you. My heart is filled with gratitude. I imagine now that it is already done and I say, "YES!" with every part of my body, mind and soul. I release this word to the law of manifestation. I know it is so. And it is done. So be it. It is done. Amen and so it is.

Prayer of Discovery (Ch. 2)

Great Oneness, Divine Intelligence, I know that I am one with the power of Love which is stronger than any other power in the universe. I surrender all fear, doubt, trepidations to the power of Love and Light. I ask from the deepest part of my being for divine guidance, clarity and courage to look and find the patterns that have been destructive in my life. I am ready, willing and able to take the action of self-inquiry. I am choosing to go into my past to find the saboteurs and patterns that have kept me small, constricted, in pain, and in emotional bondage. I ask for the help of my Higher Self and Inner Counselor to assist me with this. I thank you for this and as I release this word to the Law, I know it is done. Thank you, and so it is.

The Path to Wholeness (Ch. 6)

Divine Mother, hold me in your heart today. I open my heart so your unconditional love may flow through you to me, from heaven to earth. Let me be gentle as I walk through this day.

Let me be the love I so deeply crave so that I may bring beauty everywhere I go with my presence. Let me make time for myself to be touched by nature and allow my sensuality to open like a flower in the sunshine. Let the sweet perfume of my soul essence sweeten the air as the vibration is transformed from fear to love in moments of self-remembering.

Pivot my old thoughts of reacting from my conditioned mind to this moment of my awakened heart-mind. Awaken and open my heart to the soft whispering of love's soul song. Let me truly hear the birds as they greet life with joy.

Let my tears from letting go of the illusions purify my soul so that my light may be seen and brighten this world. Remind me to be grateful for all of the good that I have been graced with.

Please release me of the judgments that I have placed on myself and on others. These attachments feel like barnacles on my sailing vessel, they slow me down and eat the body of my soul. I release all of my separateness to you as I walk through this path of beauty today with you, shining your love and light through my heart. I know I am one with true beauty today as we leave flowers where our footsteps have been.

Thank you, thank you, thank you! And so it is, Amen.

Finding Your Treasure (Ch. 17)

Great Oneness, Divine Intelligence, I know that I am one with the power of Love, which is stronger than any other power in the universe. I surrender all fear, doubt, and trepidation to the power of Love and Light. I ask from the deepest part of my being for divine guidance, clarity and courage to look and find the patterns that have become destructive in my life. I am ready, willing and able to take the action of self-inquiry. I am choosing to go into my past to find the saboteurs and patterns that have kept me small, constricted, in pain, and in emotional bondage. I ask for the help of my Higher Self and Inner Counselor to help me with this.

Prayer for Releasing Negativity (Ch. 24)

As I connect to my own Divinity right now, which is Love, Light and Peace, I command you (insert negative emotions here) to be pulled away from my body, mind, and spirit right now. I send you to the sun NOW! Go back to the light to become beneficial energy, away from my body, mind, and spirit now! Go back to the sun. You have no power over me anymore! I am taking charge of myself and I choose love, peace and freedom, harmony, laughter, joy and health. Thank you Source! Thank you, God. Thank you Divine Intelligence. So it is. So be it. Amen. It is done!

Serenity Prayer* (Ch. 24)

God grant me the serenity to accept the things I cannot change; courage to change the things I can; and wisdom to know the difference. Amen.

* Excerpted from Alcoholics Anonymous

Prayer of Protection (Ch. 26)

I am always safe, divinely guided, directed and protected by my higher power (or whichever deity you use). I am one with love and light. Thank you, I know this is true as I accept this as so. My heart is filled with gratitude. I release this to the LAW. I am safe and so it is! (Follow this with the centering prayer, if you have time.)

Healing Prayer (Ch. 27)

I light this candle to connect with my Divinity. I ask _____ [my angels, guides and teachers; or, for me it is Jesus Christ and the Holy Spirit] to assist me in doing my inner work. I know there is only one power, one Light. I am one with Light now. As the wave surrenders to the ocean, I surrender to God within and to God who runs the universe, to the power and presence of Love that is the glue that holds the universe together. I release all fear, all worries, all doubts; all thoughts that I can't do it, all saboteurs, all parts of me that have not come to the Light yet. I now surrender you to the Light.

As I look at this candle, it represents that I am surrendered to the Light. I ask for courage. I ask for the courage to let go of what no longer serves me, the courage to open up, to accept and receive the love, the nurturing, and the connection to another person. I ask that my inner child be very present with me and my adult self has the courage to ask for what I need.

And so I know that as I ask, I am open to a deeper place of loving. I know that God is good and the universe is for me not against me. I re-establish my belief in a loving, powerful God and let go of the old beliefs of a punishing God. I open up and allow myself to receive the belief that I am worthy of the very best that Love and Light have to offer.

I ask for the courage to be able to ask for what I need. My little child joins me and I do it in a playful, loving, fun way. I ask for the courage to have eye contact so I can truly connect to another. Knowing that the universe always says "YES!" God always says, "Yes" to Love! I now release this prayer with conviction of the law of manifestation. I let it go and I say "thank you!" As I let it go, I celebrate and know that what I ask always comes back to me fulfilled. My prayer is fulfilled. So I say, "Yes!" "Thank you!" I release this word. I simply allow it to be. I now fully and completely accept it on all levels. Thank you, God! Thank you, Universe! Thank you, Love! And so it is.

Amen. So it is done.

THIRTY-THREE WAYS TO TAKE BACK YOUR POWER AND CHANGE

HEALING MODALITIES

About Dale Bach

Dale is a motivational speaker as well as an Intuitive Counselor and Licensed Agape Spiritual Practitioner. She completed the University of Santa Monica Masters program in Spiritual Psychology, and is an advanced Psych-K Facilitator. Dale's personal mission is awakening joy and activating compassion, healing, courage, strength, peace, and freedom in others.

Dale is a survivor of severe childhood abuse that created a deep belief that she was unworthy and unlovable, and left her with patterns of self-destruction and hopelessness. This history triggered periods of alcohol and drug abuse, as well as many injuries and accidents. She unconsciously invited people to continue her abusive patterns. Through relentless efforts to heal from her past, Dale learned how to take back her power, evolving from being a victim to being a strong, compassionate woman who invokes purpose and enthusiasm for living. Dale has traveled worldwide in search of deeper healing techniques to transform her life. Now, she brings these transformative healing modalities to the public through powerful prayers, healing workshops, and on-stage and online platforms.

As a Usui and Karuna Reiki Master Teacher, Dale Bach has taught Reiki nationwide and founded many Reiki Healing Circles. A two-time Emmy Award nominee make-up artist, she found herself wanting to do more healing on-set than make-up. Dale's teachers include His Holiness the Dalai Lama, Thich Nhat Hanh, Dr. Rev. Michael B. Beckwith, and many more.

Dale is a featured author of several Transformational Guided Imagery programs (TGI) through Master Key (a brain entrainment tool). Her programs combine cutting edge technology with accelerated techniques that connect the spirit to the power of the mind. These techniques offer a personal way to help release old patterns and beliefs bringing forth Authentic Self and Essential Nature.

Dale can help connect you to your own Divinity, opening the door to your soul. She ushers in healing light, enables you to see what is beyond the boundaries of your limiting beliefs, and engages your inner strength to take action! She brings health, beauty, and grace to life with her vibrant personality and genuine spirit. Expand into new possibilities, and experience profound inspiration with Dale's unique approach to guided self-realization.

Dale is now living her dream in her oceanfront cottage in San Diego, California where she boogie boards as often as she can. She has two grown daughters with whom she has beautiful loving relationships – now that she is on the other side of her own Mamma Trauma. You can learn more by visiting my website www.DaleBach.com.

I welcome your feedback!

If you have been moved by reading my book I would love to know. Your story will enrich my soul by knowing that perhaps I inspired you to heal. That perhaps it made some kind of difference in your life. I am passionate about making a difference in other people's lives and it blesses me to hear from you!

Please use my personal email address and feel free to email me as soon as you feel you have something you'd like to share:

dale@dalebach.com

More From Dale Bach

Visit www.DaleBach.com to explore and discover different healing tools available to Dale's clients around the world. You will find:

MAMMA TRAUMA book: Purchase a copy online if you would like to share this resource with a friend or family member.

MP3 Recordings of Dale's powerful prayers will help you Awaken Joy. (With original music.)

Videos: Take advantage of a special series of Videos in which Dale goes through the healing modalities in her book step by step. A great resource for anyone whose aim is to heal from Mamma Trauma.

Teleconferences: Join in a teleconference to hear from experts around the world on timely subjects that are relevant to your journey to wholeness.

Live Events: Attend one of Dale's live events. Learn how to invite Dale to speak to a women's group you belong to.

Mastermind Groups: Find out about groups that use synergy for the purpose of accelerated healing and powerful support on the journey of transformation and Awakening Joy.

Transformational Guided Imagery: Partnering with New Reality's technology and visualization techniques, Dale will help you experience positive and effective strategies for visualizing your personal goals. This is a powerful tool to help you bring about the changes you desire to experience in your life.

Therapeutic Grade Essential Oils: Use the same healing oils that Dale uses in her practice.

NOTES:

Made in the USA
Columbia, SC
06 November 2018